# Don Cupitt

*

## THE DEBATE ABOUT
# CHRIST

SCM PRESS LTD

334 00303 2

First published 1979
by SCM Press Ltd
58 Bloomsbury Street, London WC1

Filmset by Input Typesetting Ltd
and printed in Great Britain by
Fletcher & Son Ltd
Norwich

# The Debate about Christ

# Contents

# *Preface*

The conflict between Christianity's traditional doctrines and world-view on the one hand, and modern reality on the other, seems nowadays to provoke regular outbreaks of radical theology and religious controversy. In the 1950s the issue was 'demythologizing the gospel', the attempt to free Christianity from the mythological view of the world with which it has traditionally been bound up. In the 1960s the book that seemed to define the issues was Bishop John A.T. Robinson's *Honest to God,* and the main themes were the secularization of culture and the decline of belief in God. In the present decade, *The Remaking of Christian Doctrine* (1974) by Professor Maurice Wiles of Oxford focussed attention on the divinity of Christ and heralded the storm that broke over *The Myth of God Incarnate* in 1977.

The controversy is acrimonious, partly because the topic is so sensitive and partly because what is at stake this time is more than just Christianity's external compatibility with modern secular ways of thinking. It is also a matter of Christianity's internal coherence. The mainstream churches are committed to a certain doctrine about Jesus, but specialists in early Christian thought are questioning the arguments by which that doctrine was reached, New Testament scholars ask if the New Testament teaches it at all, and historians wonder at the gulf between Jesus himself and fully-developed Christianity.

These questions are very unsettling, for they imply that Christianity may be in a worse condition than was thought. It is perhaps not a basically sound structure that needs only to be modernized, but may be in need of radical reconstruction.

It is not surprising that controversy is sharp and the points of view expressed many.

The issues are by no means new. The philosopher John Locke was raising some of them as early as 1695 in *The Reasonableness of Christianity*. He says that the earliest Christian faith was simply in the messiahship of Jesus and the title 'Son of God' at first meant no more than 'Messiah', and he implies that further doctrinal elaboration is needless and harmful. During the next generation a surprising number of leading Anglicans held views close to Locke's.

This precedent reminds us of some persisting features of English religious thought which may puzzle overseas readers. The Church of England was not blessed (or cursed, as the case may be) with a strong dogmatic tradition of its own. It merely professed to believe the faith of scripture and the primitive church. There was a distrust of 'hypothesis', needlessly elaborate speculation of a kind which was supposed to have flourished in the Middle Ages, and to be still flourishing on the European mainland. In a man like Locke, the influence of empiricist philosophy and natural science combined to form a strong preference for simplicity and economy in theorizing.

At its worst English theology has perhaps been too tentative and amateurish, but at its best it has been very responsive to new ideas in philosophy, science and historical criticism, and has tried to stick closely to ascertainable facts and to moral experience.

The arguments set out and evaluated in this book have been advanced in what is so far an almost entirely British context, but I believe that their interest and importance is far wider. Technical detail and jargon has been reduced to the minimum in the hope that non-specialist readers will be able quickly to get to the heart of the argument. As the man says, Judge for yourselves what is right!

Biblical quotations are from the Revised Standard Version.

*Cambridge, November 1978*                                *Don Cupitt*

# 1

# The Meaning of the Incarnation

## 1.1 *The standard doctrine*

In the year 325, after the end of the Council of Nicea, Eusebius, Bishop of Caesarea in Asia Minor found himself in a delicate position. He had just compromised his principles and, more important, those of his church at Caesarea by accepting and signing an alteration in its baptismal Creed. The key passage used to run as follows:

[We believe in] One Lord Jesus Christ, the Word of God, God from God, Light from Light, Life from Life, Only-begotten Son, first-born of all creation, before all the ages begotten from the Father, by Whom [i.e., by the Word] also all things were made; Who for our Salvation was incarnate and lived among men. . . . [1]

This form of words may have been in use at Caesarea for half a century or more. It was a typical third-century Eastern Creed, more florid in its language than the forms of words preferred in the Latin West. It teaches the divinity of Christ, whom it calls the Word of God, but in terms which suggest that he is a subordinate divine being who links the One God with creation. The New Testament phrase 'first-born of all creation', taken literally, implies that the Word of God is a created being, the first and eldest of creatures. It is also noticeable that the old Creed of Caesarea does not explicitly teach Christ's full humanity either, for it merely says that he 'lived among men'.

At Nicea a new and altogether tighter orthodoxy was taking shape and Eusebius had found himself under heavy pressure to come into line. Writing home to Caesarea to explain and excuse his action, Eusebius claimed that the new version of the Creed was only different by one word from the old. The new word was 'consubstantial', and 'our most wise and most religious Emperor' Constantine had strongly advised all present to accept it so as to exclude the heresy of the troublesome Alexandrian priest Arius. Eusebius did accept it, which brought him back into the sunlight of imperial favour, but his letter home was less than candid. More than just one word had been changed:

[We believe in] One Lord Jesus Christ, the Son of God, begotten of the Father, Only-begotten, that is, from the substance of the Father; God from God, Light from Light, Very God from Very God, begotten not made, Consubstantial with the Father, by Whom [i.e., by the Son] all things were made, both things in heaven and things in earth; Who for us men and for our salvation came down and was incarnate, and was made man. . . .[2]

This form of words was further revised in 381 to give us the words in which the Nicene Creed is recited today, but the essential doctrine is already clear in 325 and is emphasized, not (as Eusebius claimed) by a single word, but by half-a-dozen changes which all combine to make the new doctrine crystal-clear. The 'heretic' Arius had taught, admittedly in a rather militant and provocative way, much the same doctrine as the old Creed of Caesarea: Christ was a created, subordinate divine being who linked God with the world. The new orthodoxy insisted that he was an uncreated and fully coequal divine being. From now on, the Son, being 'begotten', had a quite different status from things which were 'made', a distinction which had not been clearly made in the past.

It was a major development, but in spite of long and bitter controversies it stuck, and there was no going back on it. Ever since Nicea mainstream Christianity has believed that the incarnate Lord Jesus Christ is Very God of Very God, coequally and coeternally God. The precise meaning of the key word 'consubstantial' is a highly technical question about which volumes have been written, but for our present purpose it is sufficient to get an idea of its meaning from the half-dozen changes which were made in order to turn the Creed of Caesarea into the Creed of Nicea. In the third century there had been a tradition of saying that Christ was 'God of Very God', rather as in ancient Egypt the Pharaoh was the 'good God', as distinct from the Supreme Being, the 'Great God'. There was a linguistic distinction between God and the earthly being who represented or incarnated God. But Nicea denied *any* subordination. The incarnate God was fully coequal with the Creator, and that is the basic meaning of the divinity of Christ. The incarnate Lord is just as much God as God is God. It is true that the Father begets the Son and not the Son the Father. But this relationship of begetting is an eternal relationship, not something that occurs in time; and the Father communicates without reserve his entire divine nature to the Son so that the Son is in no respect inferior to the Father. It is true that the Father is unoriginated and the Son originated, but the two are ranked together over against everything created.

To a modern reader, no doubt, the really extraordinary thing is how Jesus of Nazareth ever came to be identified with the heavenly being who was the principle of order in the cosmos *at all*. But that first step had been taken very early. As we shall see later, St Paul had linked Jesus with the divine Wisdom in about AD 55, and St John had linked him with the divine Word in about AD 95. We noted that Jesus Christ was still being identified primarily as the *Word* of God in Caesarea up to 325.

Nicea preferred to call the cosmic being with whom Christ was identified the Son rather than the Word, because Father-Son imagery seems to make more acceptable the substance-language which follows. The Father unreservedly and eternally communicates to the Son the whole substance of his own proper being without any holding back, so that the Son is fully and coequally Very God of Very God ('Very' meaning 'true'). That was the biggest single innovation, the

claim that the Son of God is Very God. The New Testament
never suggests that the phrase 'Son of God' just means
'God'. In ancient Jewish thought sonship meant obedience to
authority, and sons were by no means equal to their fathers.
To the Jews the title 'Son of God' was a human title suggesting human piety and divine protection, and to this day Christians preserve that old meaning of the idiom when they say
the Lord's Prayer and think of themselves as becoming sons
of God through baptism. But Nicea gave the title Son of God
a new technical meaning in connection with Jesus alone:
*equality*. So in Christian idiom Jesus may be called 'God
incarnate' or 'the Son of God incarnate', and the two expressions are taken to mean the same.

Incidentally, the distinction between upper-and-lower-
case lettering was invented only in the Middle Ages. All
modern printed versions of the Bible project Nicea's doctrine
back into the text by the way they give the word 'Son' a
capital letter when it is used in connection with Jesus, and not
when it is used of angels, the King of Israel, or ordinary
believers. The same thing is done with terms like Word,
Spirit, etc.

There is a further point of idiom. The Nicene doctrine can
be defined in three propositions, each of which makes a different move:

(*i*) Jesus is the Lord Jesus Christ;

(*ii*) The Lord Jesus Christ is the Son of God; and

(*iii*) The Son of God is eternally Very God of Very God.

The first move is rather like the move from 'Elizabeth' to
'Her Majesty Queen Elizabeth the Second'. It is a move from
the mere person to the person in the full dignity of her or his
titles and role.

The second move is rather like the move from 'H.M. Queen
Elizabeth II' to 'the Crown', for the Crown does many things
in which the present monarch is not directly and personally
involved, and the Crown existed before and will presumably
exist after the span of this particular person's reign. Rather

similarly, God's Son is thought of as having existed in heaven before Jesus' lifetime, and even as continuing to uphold the cosmos *during* Jesus' lifetime. So the lifespan of the human Jesus is only one earthly episode in the heavenly life of the Son of God. The person who lived the life of Jesus is none other than the heavenly Son of God, but (to put it crudely) the Son of God's throne was not vacant before Jesus, nor was it vacant during his life.

The third move we have already discussed. It is the most controversial, and the reason why Nicea gave rise to such bitter and prolonged arguments. Many resented the doctrinal innovation, and even those who were prepared to accept it found if difficult to say how the Lord Jesus Christ was 'one' while *combining* living a fully human life in time with (again putting it crudely) being God and running the universe. Given that the Son of God is Very God of Very God, what account could be given of the human Jesus, and of the unity of Christ?

## 1.2 *Heresies excluded*

When a brother bishop heard in 444 of the death of the great theologian and saint Cyril of Alexandria he wrote feelingly about the event. 'At last the villain has gone,' he said, 'I hope his gravestone is very big and heavy, for I fear that Cyril will vex the dead so much that they will try to send him back to us.'

Remarks like that are liable to give the Church Fathers a reputation for being uncharitable. But we should not forget that it is quite possible to combine being a highly unpleasant person with being a brilliant theologian. Cyril managed it easily, and the fact is that the long controversy after Nicea is intellectually one of the most exciting in the history of religions. In a herculean effort before it perished the ancient world spent its remaining philosophical strength in defining the doctrine of Christ.

The Fathers were different from us. They differed in their assumptions. Though they emphasized the limits of human reason and human language in dealing with divine things, they nevertheless went on to define doctrines with a confidence we cannot share and to use concepts that we cannot use. In addition, they lacked our historical awareness. As theologians say, they assumed the unity of scripture and tradition, which means that in reading the New Testament they naturally and unselfconsciously read it in terms of all the ideas that had been superimposed upon it since it was written. Unlike us they felt no obligation to try to set aside their assumptions, do some historical research into first-century Palestinian Judaism, and try to understand that remote and strange world in its own terms. Where our outlook is critical, analytical and historical, their outlook was accumulative and systematic. They were building Christendom, not dissecting the past. They knew that St John's gospel is different from the other three, but it did not bother them, and they quote the words of John's Jesus as if they were quite sure that Jesus himself had spoken them all. They knew that their terminology was unscriptural and that they were saying things that the New Testament does not quite say, but it did not trouble them.

Not only were their assumptions different from ours, but their practical interests were different too. The correct definition and forcible imposition of orthodoxy (right belief) was a matter of high importance to both church and empire, rather as ideological correctness is important in a modern socialist state. Orthodoxy was defined by majority vote at large Councils against a background of violent controversy, forceful advocacy, intrigue, arm-twisting, exiling the opposi-ton, street hooliganism (led by private armies of wild monks) and the rest of the time-honoured methods of political debate. Whatever the methods used to obtain the consensus, those who lost were heretics (upholders of arbitrary opinions) at odds with consensus of the faithful.

So it had to be, though many at the time deplored the wheeling-and-dealing. St Gregory of Nazianzus wrote in 382 to excuse himself from attending yet another Council: 'My inclination is to avoid all assemblies of bishops . . . You always find there love of contention and love of power which beggar description.'

But the direction in which the debate moved was not arbitrary. The church was working out a rationale of its own position as the established church of the empire, and what was said of Christ had implications for the church's own authority and its cosmic significance. He was the only way to salvation – so it was. He linked heaven and earth – so it did. He had taken and saved human nature complete – so the church had the power to hallow all aspects of human life. He was coequally divine – so his church's authority was not one whit less than the Creator's, for Christ had given his own unqualified endorsement to the church. He was one person, divine and human – so the bridge between earth and heaven in the church was rock solid.

It followed that the orthodox faith *must* be that Christ was fully God, fully human and one person. Somehow a form of words had to be found that would say all those three things without diminishing any of them.

There had to be something in the human Jesus which would firmly lock him to the Son of God, without diminishing his humanity. You had to say that he had a human body, a human soul, even a free human will to experience temptation. So at what point could he be connected with the Son of God, in order that he can rightly be called the incarnation of the Son of God?

The answer given was that you must distinguish between our common human nature and the individualizing principle (the 'person') which makes distinct individuals of you and me. Jesus had common human nature complete, but in him the human individualizing principle, the person, was replaced by the person (Greek, *hypostasis*) of the Son of God.

Hence in traditional Christian language Jesus is always called man and not *a* man. The Son of God took human nature upon him and became man, not a man. What makes the human Jesus an individual is the person of the Son of God.

The word 'person' is not being used in its modern psychological sense. The orthodox doctrine says that Jesus has a complete human psychology. But the subject who lived the human life of Jesus is not a human subject, but the Son of God. The human Jesus is not supposed to be a glove-puppet with the hand of God inside it. He is supposed to be fully human, with human thoughts, feelings and volitions: but he is also the Son of God who has assumed or added to himself a complete human nature. The standard form of words was agreed at the Council of Chalcedon in 451:

... our Lord Jesus Christ is to us One and the same Son, the Self-same Perfect in Godhead, the Self-same Perfect in Manhood; truly God and truly Man; the Self-same of a rational soul and body; coessential with the Father according to the Godhead, the Self-same coessential with us according to the Manhood; like us in all things, sin apart; before the ages begotten of the Father as to the Godhead, but in the last days, the Self-same, for us and for our salvation (born) of Mary the Virgin God-bearer as to the Manhood; One and the Same Christ, Son, Lord, Only-begotten; acknowledged in Two Natures without confusion, change, division or separation, the difference of the Natures being in no way removed because of the Union, but rather the properties of each Nature being preserved and (both) concurring into One Person....[3]

That is orthodoxy, but there were differences of emphasis within it. Some emphasized the distinctness of the two natures of Christ, human and divine. The definition insists on their union in Christ indeed, but it unites them only in a bare metaphysical point, the 'person'. What matters empirically is the moral union of the human Jesus with God. So you could read Chalcedon as still maintaining the clear distinctness of the two natures, and not converting God into man.

Another tradition, exemplified by Cyril, emphasized that

the Word *became* flesh. Their banner was the word 'God-bearer' or Mother of God, as applied to Mary. That to which she gave birth was God's coequal Word *become flesh*. When Nestorius, Bishop of Constantinople refused to accept the word 'God-bearer' Cyril determined to have him out. In an official letter handed to Nestorius on 7 December 430, Cyril helpfully provided a list of 'points which it is necessary for your Reverence to anathematize' The first runs:

If anyone confesses not Immanuel to be God in truth and the holy Virgin on this ground to be the God-bearer, since she brought forth after the flesh the Word of God who became flesh, let him be anathema.

And the last runs:

If anyone does not confess that the Word of God suffered in flesh and was crucified in flesh and 'tasted of death' in flesh and became 'Firstborn from the dead,' inasmuch as he is Life and Life-giving, as God, let him be anathema.[4]

At one extreme – Cyril's – the incarnation is overwhelmingly a *physical* reality. Cyril is carnal. At the other extreme the incarnation is a bare metaphysical point, and becomes in practice primarily a *moral* reality. Chalcedon's form of words has elements of both points of view, so it was something of a compromise.

Cyril won that particular battle, and Nestorius was deposed. But in one form or another the struggle between Nestorius' moral view of Jesus' relation to God and Cyril's carnal view has continued.


1.3 *A modern revision*

The development of the classic doctrine of the incarnation continued for two centuries after Chalcedon though at a slower pace and in only minor details. The final construction is surely one of the grandest and strangest creations of the human mind. Christos Pantocrator, Christ Almighty, had become a figure reminiscent of the Cosmic Giant in early India, but even greater. Cosmic Godman and Lord of the universe, he embraced and joined together in his own person the God of Israel and the entire created order. Plato's Academy was shut down, after 1000 years. What space was left for autonomous reason or natural science? Where the whole universe was summed up in one divine-human person theology was the only science, theocracy the only politics, and icon-making the only art.

Oft-repeated clichés about Christian civilization down the centuries tend to create an impression of long ages of untroubled faith. But the great Christendom synthesis was never untroubled. Even as it was being put together Rome fell, and the Arabs were on the brink of converting half the Christian world to Islam by reviving the older tradition of prophetic faith. And as soon as the West struggled back out of illiteracy secular reason reasserted itself.

But in the Western Middle Ages, beside the Christ Almighty of the Doom paintings there was another and cherished image of Jesus as a humble poor man, a figure not at the top but at the bottom of the cosmic scale. He represents a different tradition of incarnational thinking, which has become increasingly important in the modern period. It draws its inspiration from St Paul's words (Philippians 2. 5f.):

Have this mind among yourselves, which you have in Christ Jesus, who, though he was in the form of God, did not count equality with God a thing to be grasped, but emptied (*ekenōsen*) himself, taking the form of a servant, being born in the likeness of men.

Strictly speaking, this passage seems not to be about the incarnation, for the one to whom the self-emptying or *kenosis* is attributed is not God, nor the Son of God, but Jesus; and St Paul presumably did not think that *the human Jesus* existed before he was born. Nevertheless, the passage is nowadays commonly interpreted of the incarnation, with emphasis on the humility of God in hiding himself in the lowly figure of

Jesus. The theory began to be important in the nineteenth century for reasons that we will come to in a moment, but it has deep roots in the past.

The two-natures Christ of Chalcedon showed his human nature in his weakness – his hunger and thirst, his temptation, sufferings and death. He showed his divine nature most clearly in his supernatural authority and powers, his mighty works and the spectacular miracles wrought in him. But men like Luther who rebelled against the imperial theocracy of Christendom sought to see divinity not in supernatural power and might but in compassion, suffering and humiliation. The Lutheran theologians were willing to predicate the divine attributes of the merely human Jesus. There is an echo here of what we noticed in Cyril of Alexandria, who was not content with the formula that the Word was *joined to* flesh because he wanted to affirm that the Word *became* flesh, and Cyril went further than most towards saying that in the incarnation the Word of God, who is Very God, experiences finitude, suffering and death. Cyril's 'carnality' reappears in 'kenotic' theories of the incarnation, theories of God's self-emptying so as to squeeze himself into a merely human Jesus.

In the nineteenth century the old Chalcedonian doctrine of Christ began to seem indefensible for reasons to do with philosophy and historical method. The entire supernatural apparatus of the gospels, on which the traditional arguments for his divinity had rested, was crumbling. A merely human Jesus was left, a man wholly committed to a very remote culture. If you wanted to go on affirming the incarnation you had to find the divine attributes in this merely human Jesus. Furthermore, nineteenth-century thought could make no sense of the old metaphysical notion of 'person', nor of the idea that the incarnate Lord had a dual consciousness (God the Son's awareness of himself as God, and the human Jesus' purely human self-awareness) in his one person. The thought of the period was liberal, humanitarian and anti-despotic. For all these reasons kenotic doctrines of Christ began to appear, and became very popular.

Early forms of the doctrine, taught by mid-nineteenth century Lutheran theologians, were highly mythological. It was said that God the Son had laid aside his divine attributes of onimpotence, omniscience and cosmic lordship in order to descend to earth as a man, a story which sounded all too like fairy tales of a king who lays aside his royal insignia so as to go about the streets incognito and perhaps woo a beggar-maid. Similar tales of the high God appearing incognito in human form are told of Zeus and Odin.

A more moderate line of thought went as follows: It is obvious from the gospels that Jesus believed in evil spirits and the world-view of Jewish apocalyptic, that he thought the world would end within a generation or so but professed ignorance of the precise date, and that he accepted Moses' authorship of Genesis, David's authorship of the Psalter and other popular but erroneous beliefs. Yet according to traditional doctrine he was infallible, his divine mind preserving his human mind from any taint of error. There was a clear contradiction here. It looked as if it had to be said that in becoming incarnate he had voluntarily limited himself so that his psychology, his knowledge and his outlook were those of a man of his time. The nineteenth century was historically minded, and people realized that actual human existence is always conditioned by history and culture. To become truly man, God the Son must take upon himself not just the outer but also the *inner* conditions of one particular time and culture. So there must be some kind of veil between the human Jesus and the omniscience of God the Son, or Jesus would not be truly human.

This line of thought has one or two disturbing implications. It begins to drive a wedge between the historical Jesus and the divine Christ of faith. Before the modern historical consciousness arose it had been assumed that the historical incarnate Lord Jesus was a figure of timeless authority, infallible for every subsequent generation. But now it was being admitted that history is a process of continuous conceptual and moral change. The historical Jesus was, to put it bluntly, inevitably obsolete and out-of-date in many respects because of the nature of history.

The effect of all this was to produce a subtle shift in the way people understood the doctrine of the incarnation. You could no longer claim to *see* the incarnation empirically manifest in the figure of the historical Lord Jesus. Instead you had to *believe* the incarnation as a hidden act of God behind the empirical Jesus. People have begun to believe the incarnation on the authority of the early church and tradition, rather than to infer it as a factual thing from the historical facts about Jesus. The incarnation does not plant an objective absolute in history, for history does not admit absolutes: what it does is reveal to all men in all times that God has taken human life into the divine life, that God has experienced the human condition, that God *is* human and suffers in man for man.

Such a view of the incarnation has been defended in the present English controversy by Brian Hebblethwaite of Queens' College, Cambridge, a young theologian in the tradition of the late Austin Farrer. Examples of his work may be found in *The Truth of God Incarnate* and *Incarnation and Myth*, both of which appear in the Further Reading list at the end of this book. His account is, he claims, free of mythology and he entirely rejects any supernaturalist account of Jesus. In the incarnation God the Son has made his own the humanity of an ordinary first-century Jewish man. No mythological 'descent' is implied. God the Son remains eternally and unchangeably God the Son. But within his infinite divine consciousness he has taken on, as one finite mode of his infinite experience, the life of the man Jesus, whose life is therefore a mode of God's life.

The human Jesus is thus truly God the Son incarnate; but being incarnate his consciousness is purely human, and within his incarnate life he experiences his eternal unity with

God the Father only in terms of human faith and prayer. In this way the human Jesus' faith in God is a human analogue of, and a real part of, the eternal communion of God the Son with God the Father. In Hebblethwaite's theology it is important that there are eternal personal relationships and values within the unity of the Godhead, and that through the incarnation man can be incorporated into the eternal divine life. For the incarnation is God's assumption or taking up of humanity into eternity.

Impressive as it is, this account is not without difficulties of its own. If, so far as facts and observables are concerned, Jesus is just an ordinary man how can we know that this account is true? What could be evidence for it? Hebblethwaite appeals to tradition, to religious experience, to the moral and religious values which it embodies, and to the testimony of the early church. He remains broadly Chalcedonian, for he still says that the subject who lives the life of Jesus is God the Son, but he has a problem in asserting the identity of the human subject Jesus with the divine subject, God the Son. Can it make sense to say that the two are the same?

That problem, the *unity* of the incarnate godman, troubles every version of the doctrine of the incarnation. The dilemma is this: Could Jesus have willed evil? If the answer is yes, he was human and not divine. If the answer is no, he was divine and not human. If the answer is yes-and-no, then he was not one person.

# 2

## Religious Difficulties

To people who are not professionally concerned with such things doctrines of the incarnation are apt to seem weirdly abstract and scholastic, having little to do with either Jesus of Nazareth or ordinary Christian living and worship. Surely, to believe that Jesus is God or the Son of God is a simple matter of accepting his authority, giving him our devotion, letting him be the guide and inspiration of our lives, and hoping that he will deliver us in the hour of death? I have met many otherwise intelligent people who just do not see what all the fuss is about.

But the whole point of the doctrine of the incarnation is that to the people who originally framed it it was surrounded by seemingly insuperable difficulties, difficulties which have never been wholly overcome.

### 2.1 *God*

The most vital problems concern the doctrine of God. We live in a time when belief in God is very weak and shadowy indeed. That does not mean that people are less religious, for it could well be that the number of people who are aware of religious needs and yearnings is greater than ever, but it does mean that people's idea of God is now so nebulous that they may seize gratefully on the claim that 'Jesus is God', as helping them to give the idea of God some content. They notice the advantages rather than the difficulties of incarnational belief: 'I don't know what God is, but this man is proferred as

an authoritative image of God in human form, and I am glad
to have that at least to cling to.'

In earlier times it was quite different. Jew, Greek and (later)
Arab were already in possession of passionately-held convictions about God which seemed to rule out the incarnation as
blasphemous nonsense. Although some Christians may have
used language that implied belief in the incarnation by the
end of the first century, they did not produce clear theories of
what they meant till the fourth century, and some would say
that a fully coherent theory has *never* been put forward.

The semitic idioms in which Jews and Arabs expressed
their basic convictions are unfamiliar now, but for them God
was an intense and overwhelming reality, the central concern
of individual and social life, utterly exalted in holiness,
sovereignty and righteousness, and in every way unique,
non-human and beyond all imagery. Man is frail and changeable flesh; God is invincible, invulnerable, unchallengable
and incomparable. God's unity and transcendence are absolute, but God is not remote, for God presses upon one in
every moment of life and is the power by which one lives or
dies. The favour of God is the highest bliss and the wrath of
God (alienation from God) is utter damnation. In times when
religious controversy was less inhibited than it is now Jews
thought of the incarnation as idolatry, and Muslims as blasphemy.

In pre-Christian times the Jews had already begun to translate their beliefs about God into the language of Greek
philosophy. It is often complained that the God of religious
experience is quite different from the God of the
philosophers, but this anxiety was not felt by men like the
Jewish philosopher of Alexandria, Philo (*c.*20 BC to *c.* AD 50),
nor by the Greek Christian Fathers who inherited his work.
The men who framed the doctrine of the incarnation worked
with a Greek idea of God which they mostly took to be a fair
representation of the faith of Israel. It went roughly like this:

Since God is not an object in the world, God cannot be

described in the ordinary way. So theologians do not usually speak of God's properties or qualities but of God's 'attributes' – things you may call God, or ways in which it is right to speak of God. God's nature is *Spirit*, which means that God's life and being are utterly unconstrained in power, creativity, wisdom and goodness by any limitations of time, change, space or bodiliness. God is said to be *incomprehensible* (beyond our powers of language and understanding); *impassible* (never sufferer or patient, but always agent); *indivisible* (absolutely simple and structureless); *self-identical* (and so wholly unchangeable); *infinite* (in no way bounded or constrained); and utterly *holy* (pure, separate, exalted and other than man).

This language may seem strange and highflown, but if for a moment a modern man can suspend his habitual disbelief and think what it might be really to believe in a God so spoken of, then he may see what an extraordinary and outrageous idea the incarnation of God in man is. It seems a contradiction, because the seven attributes just italicized cannot possibly be applicable to an historical human being, whoever he is. How can you reconcile the impassiblity of God with the suffering of the incarnate Lord, or the unchangeableness of God with the claim that God became incarnate on a particular day?

The two views of the incarnation that we have already discussed are related to this problem. The more cautious Chalcedon tradition says that the two natures must be kept distinct, for it would be a nonsense to fuse them together. Godness and manhood are conjoined only in the metaphysical point of the 'person' of God the Son. He, as incarnate, has two distinct natures. They may in some degree interpenetrate or inter-communicate, but belief in God is entirely based on a radical disjunction between Creator and created, and not even the incarnation can wipe out that fundamental distinction. If it did, then Christianity would slide into a soggy pantheism merging God into the world and the world into God. So even in the incarnation the distinctness of God and man must be maintained. The picture of Jesus Christ as 'two natures in one person' seems to present him as a Jekyll and Hyde, a rather grotesque dual being; but people were forced into it by their prior convictions about God and the distinction between God and the world.

The alternative view, which I called carnal and traced back from modern kenotic theories to men like Luther and Cyril, is more radical. It says – in its more extreme forms – that God really became flesh. Incarnation *means* the enfleshment of God and is the primary datum of Christianity, so that if necessary we may and must go on to revise the doctrine of God. Brian Hebblethwaite, for example, is willing to speak of the humanity and suffering of God. God has made being human, being flesh, finitude and suffering part of his own experience. Furthermore, Hebblethwaite also says that the doctrine of the incarnation is connected with the doctrine of the Trinity. For the prayers of the incarnate Lord are a revelation in human terms of eternal loving personal relationships within the Trinity, to which human beings can be admitted through Christ. All this implies a considerable revision of the doctrine of God.

For the first school of thought God comes first, and the problem is to give an account of the incarnation which is compatible with true faith in God. But for the second school of thought the incarnation comes first, and may well oblige us to revise our view of God. A truly Christian doctrine of God will be governed and shaped by the fact of the incarnation.

This second approach naturally has a strong appeal today when, as we noted, so many people are decidedly vague about God and respond gratefully to the suggestion that God is like Jesus. However, in an age as atheistic as ours people may easily move on to conclude: 'I can safely forget about the old God; it's enough to worship the man Jesus as God.' In the 1960s some people put forward a still more extreme version of this, under the label of Christian Atheism. Christianity was turned into a non-religious following of Jesus as hero. What would Jesus himself have thought of that?


## 2.2 *The freedom of Jesus*

All doctrines of the incarnation that deserve consideration say *both* that Jesus is fully human with a free human will, *and* that the subject who lived his life is the divine Son of God. But if these two statements contradict each other, then the incarnation-doctrine cannot be true, because it is logically incoherent. It does not hang together, because it contains an internal self-contradiction.

The problem is that the sense in which God is called free is quite different from the sense in which a human being is called free. God is called free in the sense that his purposes cannot fail. His will is all-powerful and in no way constrained or challenged. God's goodness and wisdom are perfect. So God logically cannot experience temptation, commit sin, make mistakes through lack of information or do anything but what his perfect goodness prescribes. If God says, 'I will become incarnate and save men', then nothing can stop it happening. If the subject who lived Jesus' life is God of God, then Jesus' mission cannot fail, and nothing was at risk in Jesus' life.

On the other hand religious thought *also* wants to credit Jesus with normal human freedom, which must include vulnerability to temptation, mistakes and physical constraint. The evangelists see Jesus' faith, obedience and voluntary acceptance of martyrdom as meritorious and as an inspiring example to his followers. He might have succumbed to temptation, but did not. Man's salvation was not a foregone conclusion, but was really at risk in Jesus' spiritual conflicts.

Theologians recognize the gap between God (who necessarily does right) and the human Jesus (who in spite of temptation freely chooses to do what is right), and they try to close the gap a little by ascribing all sorts of special graces to the human Jesus. But there is more to it than that, for a human being's moral achievement is threatened, not only by his own weakness of will, but by many other contingencies. A tile might have dropped off the temple roof and knocked Jesus on the head. He might have decided not to call Judas, or Judas not to betray him. Pilate might have decided to avoid making a martyr of Jesus by sending him into comfortable exile to die at a ripe old age.

Thus it is very difficult to see how one can conceive the *complete immersion* of God in the changes and chances of history while God yet remains God; and how one can say that God the Son was the subject who lived Jesus' life while yet Jesus' obedience and martyrdom were humanly praiseworthy. There is no merit in a victory that was foreordained.

We feel this uncertainty in reading the gospels, and perhaps especially St Mark's passion-story. Is this the unfolding of a sacred drama predestined from all eternity? If so, one might applaud the author, but praising or blaming Judas, Peter, Pilate, Jesus and the rest seems a little beside the point. Or is it a human tragedy, with the usual mixture of noble and ignoble, error, disaster, and grief? How do we reconcile the two viewpoints, and what of the words about Judas (Mark 14.17-21)?

### 2.3 *Why only one incarnation?*

For 300 years freethinkers have used a favourite argument against Christianity which runs as follows: God is supposed to be perfectly wise and just and all-powerful. He is also supposed to offer eternal happiness or salvation to those who believe and do the right things. Being just, God must surely give every human being a fair chance of salvation. If there is something everyone must know to be saved, then God must make everyone aware of it.

But no religious system or revelation has ever been broadcast to the whole of mankind. Christianity claims that the only way to salvation is through Jesus Christ. Yet he appeared relatively late in the history of the human race, and the Christian message has only been preached to a minority – quite a small minority – of all the human beings who have ever lived. It does not make sense to say that a just God will examine the whole human race at the Last Judgment by a Christian standard, when only a minority of the candidates have had a chance to read the set book. The whole idea of a revelation, within just one cultural tradition and at one moment in time, of something necessary for *universal* salvation is absurd.

Believers have usually made two points in reply to this. They say it is possible for people outside the scope of the Christian gospel to be saved by a kind of implicit, latent or unconscious faith without actually knowing the name of Jesus. This idea was first applied to the Old Testament heroes of faith, but is nowadays extended more widely because people like the great mystics of Islam and India are obviously comparable with Christian mystics and saints. However, this concession – that there can be salvation by being a virtual Christian unawares – does not remove the great advantage of those who are explicitly in possession of the full truth. And what about a Jewish saint who has expressly *rejected* Christian claims and yet still shows the highest degree of wisdom and holiness?

Secondly, believers have suggested that God judges people who have heard the gospel by the standard of the gospel, and everyone else by such light as they have. This idea of two standards at the Last Judgment is a little incongruous, and can lead to such practical oddities as the famous occasion when the Scottish General Assembly decided not to send out missionaries to the heathen because hearing the gospel would, if they rejected it, have the unfortunate effect of *reducing* their chances of salvation!

Both these replies by the believers seem then to be rather feeble, and rather patronizing in their attitude to the 'non-Christian' world. Today the freethinkers' challenge makes us

ask, 'If it is true that God has become incarnate once, why not
more often? Various Indian traditions believe in several
incarnations, occurring at times when the world's state is
poor and deliverance is urgently needed. Why not? Why
should not God have become incarnate at least once in each
major cultural tradition – India, China, America and so on?'

Catholic and other orthodox theologians have been willing
to concede that there may be incarnations of the Word of God
in other rational species elsewhere in the universe. But no
one is willing to allow multiple incarnations of the Word or
Son of God in human form.

The reason has to do with Christianity's apocalyptic
origins. Apocalypse (Greek for 'revelation') is strictly speaking a kind of writing based on the belief that the Last Day is
very close. The writer professes to reveal the great events that
are about to happen and encourages the persecuted faithful
to hold out by promising that very soon they will be dramati-
cally vindicated. Among the Jews of Jesus' time such hopes
were strong, in some quarters at least. One of the signs that
the End was near was thought to be the appearance of a great
prophet, a new Moses or Elijah. To this day orthodox Jews
keep a vacant chair for Elijah at the Passover meal in case he
appears. Another thing expected to happen at the end was
the arrival of the Messiah, or anointed King of Israel, a
David-like figure who would return to deliver the nation
rather as in English legend it is promised that Arthur will
return in the time of the nation's need. Jesus shared many of
these ideas, and may also have expected the descent from
heaven of a superhuman figure called the Son of Man.

All such ideas are called 'eschatological', which means
'having to do with the Last Things', and apocalyptic is simply
the most dramatic and spectacular form of eschatological
hope. The main apocalyptic writings in the Bible are the
books of Daniel and Revelation, and a short apocalypse put
on Jesus' lips in Mark 13. But apart from these specifically
apocalyptic writings, most books of the New Testament con-

tain some apocalyptic or other eschatological ideas. Christianity still shows their influence in its very name, for the basic Christian affirmation about Jesus was from the first, and still is, not that he is God but that he is the Christ (Greek for 'anointed one', or Messianic King).

So the fundamental reason why Christianity will only admit one incarnation is that from the first it identified Jesus as an eschatological figure, the deliverer appointed by God who comes at the End of the world. He is final, the Last Man as St Paul calls him, and there can be no other after him. Even in the Chalcedonian Definition, quoted earlier, (1.2, above) we notice in the middle of all the Greek metaphysics that the incarnation is still said to occur 'in the last days' (the word *eschatōn* is used). Although the first intensity of expectation began to fade as early as the fifties, it died away only very slowly. In our creeds it is still said that 'he shall come again with glory to judge both the quick and the dead,' an event originally expected very soon. And believers affirm that they expect 'the resurrection of the dead and the life of the world to come', which refers to the rising of the dead and the arrival of the millenium *on this earth*. The 'world to come' is a new era of this world, not another sphere of existence.

These old apocalyptic and eschatological ideas are immensely powerful and fascinating. Every theologian wants to try to do something with them. But the last front-rank thinker to take them literally was Sir Isaac Newton, 250 years ago. They linger on in small sects and in some parts of the Third World, because of their profound appeal to the deprived. I admire them myself, and want to salvage something from them, but they are not literally true.

Now Newton still thought the Bible had been as good as written by God, and he thought that God governed the course of history according to the principles of the books of Daniel and Revelation. But if we ask ourselves today, 'Does the Eternal God think in the categories of Jewish apocalyptic?', the answer is obviously, 'No! The idea is absurd.' To cite

Christianity's apocalyptic origins and its belief that Jesus was mankind's last chance before the End of all things, is to give a *historical* reason why theologians will not admit other incarnations. But it is no good as *theological* reason, unless you really think you can prove that God is and acts as described in ancient apocalyptic belief.

So we have still not found a good answer to the question, 'Why only one incarnation?' It is a question that presses particularly hard on the sort of modern kenotic theory that I linked with the name of Brian Hebblethwaite. For he is modern and critical. He admits the historical obsoleteness of many of Jesus' ideas, and the limitations of Jesus' knowledge. He expressly says that God became a first-century Jew, locked into that particular cultural setting. But the obvious implication of all this is that the power and relevance of the incarnation of God in Jesus only lasts as long and only extends as far as Jesus' outlook and ways of speaking are intelligible. He cannot reach the whole human race.

Hebblethwaite has a reply. He says that the truths *about God* which the incarnation reveals are universal. So even though the range of *the man Jesus* is limited, incarnational theology stretches far beyond it and can make sense to everyone at all times. A fair reply, but it still has the effect of separating incarnational theology a little from the man Jesus. And we can still say, 'Why should not the great truths about God to which incarnational theology bears witness be re-embodied in many human lives? God the Son is supposed to be infinite, and so presumably has the power to adopt any number of finite human lives into and as his own. Why hasn't he done so?'

## 2.4 *Is it a contradiction?*

From time to time it has been asserted that the doctrine of the incarnation is formally self-contradictory, because the one person of the incarnate Lord Jesus Christ is credited with possessing two lists of attributes which at point after point contradict each other.

The difficulty goes back to Plato, who defined the earthly and heavenly worlds as opposites – the former changeable, imperfect, and never fully real, and the latter unchangeable, perfect, eternal and wholly real. Later, the same contrasts passed into the Greek doctrines of God and man. Then when it began to be said that Jesus Christ was the Godman he was called upon to unite the opposites. As God he was unchangeable, all-knowing, all-powerful, perfect and incapable of suffering; but as man he was changeable, ignorant, weak, finite and afflicted. And yet it was insisted that he was one person, who simultaneously and without prejudice to his perfect unity was both infinite and finite, incapable of temptation and capable of temptation, and so on. If such claims are formally self-contradictory then the doctrine of the incarnation cannot be true. It is nonsense.

Some theologians have held that the classic doctrine is self-contradictory, and Professor John Hick would perhaps wish to join them. The orthodox tend to reply that it is not contradictory because it is revealed truth, and God cannot lie; but it passes our comprehension and so may be dubbed a mystery or a paradox.

I am inclined to agree with the orthodox here, for two reasons. The first is that in theology a great many of the key words are always used in stretched or analogically-extended senses. Thus, God is not infinite in the mathematical sense, but in a special sense. God is not powerful in the political sense, nor in the physical sense, but in a special sense. And so on; for all the key words used in speaking of God are inevitably used in special, rather mysterious ways, because God is not part of the world and does not resemble anything in the world. We do not fully understand and cannot strictly define any of the key words we use in speaking of God. But we can only say with complete confidence that two statements contradict each other if we are quite sure of the meanings of both of them, and in theology meanings are not that clear. So I am reluctant to claim that the things said about Jesus as the Godman are self-contradictory, though I do think they *seem* to be so.

Secondly, the appeal to paradox and mystery is not always a piece of sleight-of-hand. For there are many things in human life which have proved, so far at least, to be insolubly mysterious. The relation of mind and body, and the problem of human freedom, are two of them. I believe we are free, though I cannot fully understand how it is possible; so at this point I have to admit a paradox. Hence I have to admit that the incarnation could conceivably be another paradoxical truth, though one ought (as a matter of intellectual virtue) not to admit more paradoxes than one must.

## 2.5 *The Trinity*

If the doctrine of the incarnation goes, people say, the doctrine of the Trinity goes with it. But the doctrine of the Trinity is the distinctive Christian insight into the nature of God. So it must be retained.

It is true that the doctrine of the Trinity was developed in the decades immediately following the Council of Nicea in AD 325, and many of the arguments used in support of the coequal divinity of Christ were adapted to prove also the coequal divinity of the Holy Spirit. There was one extra difficulty in the case of the Spirit: in the case of Christ a real distinction between Jesus and God the Father is given from the outset, but what reason was there for postulating any real distinction between God the Father and God's Spirit? Surely God just *is* Spirit: Spirit is the traditional word for expressing the sovereign living energy and freedom of the divine natrure. To say that God's Spirit is a distinct Person of the Godhead seems very artificial and odd.

The word 'Trinity' is not found in the New Testament. The most trinitarian passage in the Authorized (King James) Version of the Bible, I John 5.7, is spurious and is omitted in all modern translations. Setting that aside, does a coherent account of the Spirit and the Spirit's relation to God emerge from the New Testament? Most scholars doubt it. 'Spirit' is used of the human spirit, of spirit in general, and of the divine Spirit. We hear of God's Spirit, of the Spirit of Christ, and of the Holy Spirit. There is certainly an abundance of idioms, and a great deal is said. Does it all have a logic coherent enough to persuade us that the New Testament writers believed in the distinct personality (or 'hypostasis') of *the* Holy Spirit? This is a delicate question of literary and logical analysis, but I think the answer is no. Spirit idioms are used in a whole variety of ways to suggest God's self-awareness, life, activity, power, energy, self-communication, indwelling and inspiration, and are closely associated with Christ; but they are not sufficiently tightly-organized to suggest that 'the Spirit' is the proper name of a distinct coequal person of God alongside the Father and the Son.

The developed doctrine is equally puzzling. As everyone who has read the Athanasian Creed will have noticed, the logical rules governing how we should think about the Trinity are so framed that as soon as anything definite is said another rule is brought forward cancelling it. The most confusing instance is this: we may think of the Father as Creator, the Son as Redeemer and the Spirit as Sanctifier, *but we must not so think!* For God is one, and not a committee of three with distinct functions. God's works are not to be shared out among the three persons. But this removes any basis in experience for believing in the Trinity at all, for it forbids us to discriminate the persons.

It is not surprising that most Christians have always found the doctrine unusable. Attempts have been made to make it seem more reasonable by claiming that in other religions analogous insights are found. But the examples quoted (from Egypt, India, neo-Platonism and so on) will not bear close examination. It is more to the point that the main tradition of

monotheism, stemming from the Israelite prophets and
Zoroaster, has nowhere else but in Christianity felt the need
for such a doctrine.

Why then did Christianity take this route? The main factor
is the influence of the New Testament formula, the Father,
the Son and the Holy Spirit, the threefoldname mentioned
in Matthew 28.19, II Corinthians 13.14 and elsewhere.
Nobody thinks Matthew's formula goes back to Jesus himself,
because the earliest baptism seems to have been in the name
of Jesus only, and Matthew's words presume the existence of
an organized church with a settled pattern of instruction for
converts. But clearly there *was* baptism in the threefold name
from quite early times. Why?

Theologians distinguish two kinds of doctrine of the Trinity, 'essential' and 'economic'. An essential Trinity grounds
the threefoldness in God's eternal being. God absolutely is in
some way Three in One and One in Three. An economic
Trinity grounds the threefoldness in revelation and the history of salvation. We do not presume to suggest any absolute
threefoldness in God, for we have no basis for speaking about
God absolutely. We know God only in his dealings with us.
So an economic trinity-doctrine confines itself to saying that
there is a sort of threefoldness in salvation.

This last line of thought suggests an interpretation of the
primitive threefold name. It is not a list of three coequal,
coeternal divine persons, but a symbol of a particular form of
experience of salvation, in which God and God's Man are
united by God's Spirit. Christ is the original, the archetype,
but all believers are to participate in it. It is his baptism, and
through him the reality into which all believers are baptized.
God's Spirit is not a second person of God, but simply God's
living presence and power as experienced by human beings.
God's Son is not a second coequal person alongside God the
Father, but simply Man 'filled' with God, united with God.
So Jesus brings the threefold name: he introduced a way to

salvation in which the believer is united with God by God's own Spirit.

In this way I claim that the religious values which underlie the doctrine of the Trinity can be brought out and can be conserved without the impossibly-paradoxical doctrinal superstructure later built over them.

Others would disagree very sharply. In particular, there is an English personalist tradition going back nearly a century, which says that the importance of the doctrine of the Trinity lies in its affirmation of the ultimate and eternal significance of the personal. In God there is something analogous to personality and personal relationships. The other higher religions end in bare monotheism or in impersonal mysticism, but Christianity's unique contribution is that it points to the ultimate identity of religious and personal values (8.6, below).

# 3

# Bursting the Boundaries

## 3.1 *Christendom*

Christendom, as an entire civilization based on Christian doctrine, is usually reckoned to have lasted from the establishment of the church in the fourth century to the Reformation. But the basic doctrinal scheme of Christendom was already beginning to take shape in St Paul, and was surprisingly little affected by the Reformation. It was still widely believed in the nineteenth century and has only recently faded from the common memory.

In eternity God originally created a round number of spiritual beings, the angels. Every individual angel was a distinct species and there were nine orders of them, the whole society being a perfect living work of art. But the greatest and most beautiful angel of all, Lucifer or Satan, rebelled against God in the instant of his creation and incited many others to join him. By the will of God and the leadership of Michael the loyal angels expelled the rebels from Heaven, thereby creating a new dark world named Hell. There was now a great divide between two worlds, God's Heaven and Satan's Hell, and a large number of empty places in Heaven.

To put matters right God created a third world, Earth, intermediate between Heaven and Hell. Unlike Hell, where there is no change and Heaven, where there is neither time nor change, Earth is a world of both time and change, and is receptive to influence from the other worlds above and below it. On Earth God set Adam and Eve, specially created as adult human beings, with the intention that their descendants would eventually fill the vacant places in Heaven. And God gave them one absolute negative commandment to obey: they were to remain innocent and not to seek knowledge.

Satan was envious, and persuaded Adam and Eve to break God's commandment. They were expelled from Paradise and a curse was laid on each of them. They had lost their original righteousness and were no longer naturally destined for Heaven, but for Hell. They have since transmitted the stain and the guilt of their original sin to all their descendants through sexual intercourse. The whole of mankind has thus inherited a corrupt human nature which justly deserves God's condemnation.

But God still intended to achieve his original purpose and prepared a people, the Jews, to be the means of its fulfilment. To them was given the Law, a revelation of the divine Will, and to them in the fullness of time God sent his eternal Son who took human nature in the womb of Mary. Jesus alone of all the human race was free of all defect of either original sin or personal sins, and only he could offer to God the perfect sacrifice for the sins of all mankind. This he did on the cross, and God showed his acceptance of Jesus' sacrifice by raising Jesus from the dead and exalting him to a heavenly throne.

God's anger with sinners was now appeased and his justice satisfied. Through participation in Jesus' sacrifice all the elect could obtain the forgiveness of sins and one of the vacant places in heaven. Its efficacy was so great that it availed even for the dead, for on the Saturday that his body lay in the grave Jesus had descended to the Underworld to liberate the Old Testament prophets and other devout men who had died waiting for his coming. Finally, before leaving earth for his heavenly throne Jesus had commissioned the church, a divine society on earth which would replace Israel. The church would be animated by the Third Person of the Trinity, the Holy Spirit.

The church was the central institution in the whole of cosmic history and its earthly authority was almost boundless. Those who were baptised into it, kept its faith and persevered in obedience to its commands could hope for a place in the world to come. When God's purpose in history was complete all the dead would be raised bodily from the grave and the whole of humanity would be assembled for the Last Assize. The elect, whose number matched the number of vacant places in Heaven, would be led off to life eternal and the reprobate, the great majority of the human race, would be sealed for ever in Hell-fire. The sealing of Hell would mark God's final victory over evil and would be the occasion of great joy in Heaven. The cosmos would then be restored to the perfection God intended for it, and there would be no more change. There would be only the timeless joy of Heaven and the everlasting torment of the damned.

The whole of this cosmic drama was predestined by God's eternal decree, for predestination is not just a Calvinist idea but mainstream Christian orthodoxy, following from the doctrines of God's unconditional sovereignty, wisdom and justice. The elect are not saved by their own merits nor even by God's foreknowledge of their merits, but solely because he destined them for salvation through Christ in order to fulfil his purpose of perfecting creation.

So if someone says that he is a traditional orthodox Christian believer then *that* is what he believes, give or take a few minor differences of emphasis.

The whole doctrinal epic has some cosmological implications. It envisages a three-layered cosmos arranged in order of perfection with the bad world at the bottom, the mixed and changing world of Earth in the middle, and the perfect world at the top. But it was not, as is often thought, a flat-earth cosmology, for before the rise of Christianity the first cosmological revolution had already established a mathematical model for the motions of the planets about a fixed spherical earth. Christendom therefore envisaged the universe as a series of concentric spheres rotten at the core and becoming more perfect as one moved further out from the centre. Satan and his kingdom of Hell were located in the bowels of the

Earth at the centre of the universe. The intermediate world of men stretched from the surface of the earth to the orbit of the moon. This was the focal point of interest for all inhabitants of the cosmos, for the course of human history was the only real change going on anywhere. Both Heaven and Hell watched it with bated breath and intervened to stir things up, rather as nowadays the Superpowers make alliances and fight each other by proxy in the Third World.

Above the moon stretched the heavens of the various wandering heavenly bodies – perfect, unchangeable and highly populous regions – and then the visible creation was rounded off by the sphere of the fixed stars. Beyond was God in the Empyrean Heaven outside space and time.

The cosmos was intricate, highly-wrought and bounded in time and space. Different physical principles applied in different regions of it. For example, in the visible heavens motion was natural, everlasting and circular, whereas on earth it was produced artificially and was linear.

On earth there were no clear conceptions of magnetism or gravity. The upper hemisphere was mainly land and Jerusalem was at the centre of it, because Christ's cross had naturally been planted on the axis of the world. From this sacred centre radiated the continents of Europe, Africa and Asia. The process of Christianization spread slowly across them like a circular ripple. The lower hemisphere of water was not fit for human habitation, though Purgatory might aptly be assigned to the Antipodes.

If a modern could be suddenly translated back into the world of Christendom he would receive many unpleasant surprises. The common man's view of life would seem to be pervaded by magical and animistic beliefs and very pessimistic, being overshadowed by thoughts of sin, ritual pollution, the brevity of future history, the sorrows of this life, the certainty of judgment and the terrors of Hell. The past would appear shining and glorious, the present sadly decayed, and the future fearful. Life would be harsh and cruel, especially for children, lepers, and the insane. Society would seem prone to fits of hysteria, enthusiasm and mob violence, especially in the towns, where the crime rate was many times greater than today. Extreme squalor and a life ravaged by disease were the lot of most, and life expectancy at birth was less than half what it is now. The relative prosperity and stability of Roman times was not regained until the eighteenth century, and to keep their numbers up town populations needed continuous replenishment from the countryside until the nineteenth century.

Although Christendom's beliefs and view of the world now seem very odd indeed, the fact is that the whole scheme seemed at the time to have an impregnably-strong intellectual basis. The cosmology was not primitive but proto-scientific, and the historical scheme was consistent with the best-available authors and information. Though life was harder than we can readily imagine, the magnificence of the church and her faith gave glimpses of glories and beauties equally far beyond our present range of experience.

But Christendom's world-picture is now irrevocably shattered. We will briefly sketch six areas in which it has broken down.

## 3.2 *The Copernican revolution*

Imagine the universe as a circular theatre. All the denizens of the cosmos are arranged in ring upon ring of ascending tiers of seats, gazing down at the tiny stage on which is being enacted the drama of human history. Each act of the drama, or 'dispensation' as it used to be called, ends with a climactic event creating the conditions for the next act. The Paradisal age ends with the expulsion of our first parents from Eden, the prehistoric age of the earliest patriarchs with the Flood and the rainbow, and the age of the Patriarchs of Israel with bondage in Egypt and the exodus led by Moses. Then the age of the Law unfolds, and already two-thirds of historical time are past. Finally the incarnation begins the years of grace, the last period of universal history.

The medieval universe was big, 125 million miles across; and it was not men but angels who were the principal created intelligent beings. Still, the universe was organized around the Christian redemption-drama, and not only was it finite and built in concentric circles round man and his history, it was also hierarchically-ordered. A scale of values was built into it and human moral choice had cosmic significance, for it led one in the end either up the ladder to Heaven or down the slope to Hell.

As for Christ's work, the mythological language of the creeds seemed literally true. The divine Son had really descended through the heavens to Earth, the cockpit, the front line of the battle between Heaven and Hell. He had descended still further in order to harrow Hell, an event whose traces Dante saw, and then had ascended far above all heavens to sit enthroned over the whole cosmos.

In that world-view the religious imagery of humiliation and exaltation, descent and ascent, the ethical imagery of the lofty and the base, and the purely spatial meanings of up and down were all amalgamated.

Nicholas Copernicus' alternative system was not wholly original, for one or two people had anticipated it in a speculative way; and it did not immediately cause a great fuss. The Pope approved an outline of Copernicus' ideas in 1531. Luther, a contemporary, was neither shaken nor much impressed. It took a long time to prove the new system and to grasp its implications.

Copernicus put the Sun at the centre of the world, making the Earth describe a very large orbit around it. But the relative positions of the fixed stars appear to the naked eye to be the same all the year round. So for Copernicus the fixed stars must be very remote, and the size of the universe was multiplied by a factor of 2000. Yet it was still a bounded universe.

In 1576 Thomas Digges moved a stage further, suggesting

that 'The orbe of starres fixed *infinitely* up extendeth hit self.'[5] In the same year the visionary Dominican friar Giordano Bruno broke with orthodox Christianity, fled his Naples priory, and became the fugitive apostle of a new kind of Copernican religion until the Inquisition caught, imprisoned and finally burnt him in Rome on 17 February 1600.

Bruno was the first to realize imaginatively the consequences of the Copernican revolution. The outer walls of the medieval universe were broken and the fixed stars scattered across infinite space. Our sun was merely one star among others, with the implication that all or most of the stars were surrounded by systems of planets populated with rational beings. Bruno believed in an infinite number of inhabited worlds. The universe has no centre, and no absolute up or down. An infinite universe is relativistic, in the sense that *any* point in it may be regarded as the centre. We think ourselves central, and another species elsewhere in the universe may with as much reason consider themselves central, but there cannot be any absolute centre. No part of the universe is more or less perfect than any other, for such conceptions are merely relative to ourselves. So Heaven and Hell go off the map.

Bruno did not shrink from the obvious religious conclusions. The traditional theology that gave man a unique and privileged place in cosmic history was mistaken. Bruno rejected revealed religion, the entire biblical salvation-history, and the view of God and the God-man relationship that went with it. On the positive side, he had begun to transfer the attributes of God – infinity, fecundity, eternity, indestructibility – to the universe itself. People call him a 'pantheist', for whom God is the 'substantial form' of the universe. What that means is that Bruno can no longer believe in the Jewish God and a local incarnation in past earthly history. For him the infinite, multifarious universe is itself the plenary incarnation or self-expression of God.

A few years after Bruno's death, Galileo's telescope

revealed mountains on the moon, the satellites of Jupiter, the rings of Saturn and uncountable new stars. Newton finally sealed the triumph of the new world-picture in 1687.

Newton himself was somehow able to combine his philosophy of Nature with a biblical and Christian view of salvation-history. It is true that he and his associates had difficulty with the doctrines of the Trinity and the incarnation, but that was mainly for reasons of exegesis. Newton still thought that the God of Moses and the God of the new universe were one and the same. There is no reason in strict logic why the new world-view should be taken as falsifying the old religious picture of man's place in the universe. Maybe the Creator of a universe sixteen billion light-years across *is* primarily interested in the thoughts and deeds of human beings. Maybe he did create galaxies we shall never see for the sheer pleasure of making them, and maybe the central event in the whole of the billions of years of cosmic history is the Creator's incarnation in Jesus of Nazareth. But ever since Bruno many people have sensed a certain incongruity.

## 3.3 *Space*

On the same day in the year 1833 the two brothers Newman arrived back in England from overseas. John Henry landed from Sicily full of zeal to catholicize the Church of England and destined for fame as a writer, a Catholic convert and eventually a Cardinal. His younger brother Francis William, Fellow of Balliol, was academically the more brilliant. He returned chastened, and destined for agnosticism and an obscure career as an orientalist. Francis had been to Persia, on a missionary expedition led by an eccentric peer and Plymouth Brother named Congleton. An interesting anecdote in Francis' autobiography suggests why the enterprise was such a failure:

While we were at Aleppo, I one day got into religious discourse with a Mohammedan carpenter, which left on me a lasting impression. Among other matters, I was peculiarly desirous of disabusing him of the current notion of his people, that our gospels are spurious narratives of late date. I found great difficulty of expression; but the man ... waited patiently till I had done, and then spoke to the following effect: 'I will tell you, sir, how the case stands. God has given to you English a great many good gifts. You make fine ships and sharp penknives, and good cloth and cottons; and you have rich nobles and brave soldiers; and you write and print many learned books: ... all this is of God. But there is one thing that God has withheld from you and has revealed to us; and that is, the knowledge of the true religion by which one may be saved.'

Francis Newman's intellectual honesty, capacity for doubt and ability to take another religion seriously seemed novel and shocking. Matthew Arnold wrote that Francis was a 'beast', who seemed to think that 'enquiries into articles [of faith], biblical inspiration, etc. etc. were as much the natural functions of man as to eat and copulate'.

Traditional Christianity had always been quite uncompromising in its attitude to other faiths. It fought the Jews in its cradle. In the second century it warmly welcomed pagan philosophy but abominated pagan religion. The more closely the sacraments of paganism paralleled its own baptism and eucharist, the more it was convinced that they must be demonic parodies. It took over pagan feasts and holy places not by way of affirming continuity but in order to smother all memory of them.

As for Islam, the classic Christian view is well illustrated by the eleventh-century French epic *The Song of Roland*. Muslims are polytheists who worship images of a trinity of devils, Mahound, Termagant and Apollyon. When Charlemagne retakes Saragossa from them this is what happens:

Some thousand French search the whole town, to spy
Synagogues out and mosques and heathen shrines.
With heavy hammers and with mallets of iron
They smash the idols, the images they smite,
Make a clean sweep of mummeries and lies,
For Charles fears God and still to serve Him strives.
The Bishops next the water sanctify;

Then to the font the Paynim folk they drive.
Should Carlon's orders by any be defied
The man is hanged or slain or burned with fire.
An hundred thousand or more are thus baptized
And christened, – only the Queen fares otherwise:
She's to go captive to fair France by and by,
Her would the King convert by love to Christ. [6]

In *The Song of Roland* two different worlds clash uncomprehendingly, each closed and quite unable to understand the other. 'Paynims are wrong, Christians are right', says Roland, and that is that.

The process by which Europeans came to a better knowledge of cultures and religious belief-systems quite different from their own was very slow and long-drawn-out. Between the fifteenth and nineteenth centuries they explored almost the whole globe and a flood of travel literature was published. Sceptics would quote the different customs and beliefs of other peoples by way of teasing the Christians. But as an *argument*, this does not achieve much. The mere fact that somebody else's beliefs are different from mine does nothing to prove that my beliefs are wrong. It may only fire me with zeal to go and deliver him from his error. John Locke, in 1690, remarked that

... there is much more falsehood and error among men, than truth and knowledge. And if the opinions and persuasions of others, whom we know and think well of, be a ground of assent, men have reason to be Heathens in Japan, Mahometans in Turkey, Papists in Spain, Protestants in England, and Lutherans in Sweden.

But Locke did not conclude that Christianity was merely one local religion among many others; only that the rational man must be careful about uncritically accepting local assumptions and customs. He still thought Christianity (in a very liberal version) was the simple truth, and he never felt seriously threatened by another religion

Things became a little more serious soon afterwards, when the first translation of Confucius was published in the West.

Sceptics like Matthew Tindal could say without fear of contradiction that an eighteenth-century gentleman who read
Confucius and Moses side-by-side could not fail to prefer the
former. Confucius made Moses seem very odd indeed. Men
were bound to take other faiths more seriously when they
could read the sacred texts for themselves. George Sale's
English version of the *Koran* appeared as early as 1734.

Still, the process of understanding was very slow, and it is
perhaps only in the last hundred years that we in the West
have begun to know other faiths really well.

What is the effect on the doctrine of the incarnation? As in
the case of cosmology, there is no knock-down logical argument. It could still be the case that the incarnation of God in
Christ is a fact, that Christianity is true, and that all other
faiths are of value only in so far as they approach the full
Christian truth. But against such traditional certainties we
have to set the accumulated weight of a large number of
considerations. To the historian it looks as if Christianity is
but one religious and cultural tradition among others, some
of them at least comparable with it in their religious weight,
diversity and range of achievement. It may transpire that the
incarnation-doctrine is not an original datum in Christianity,
but a secondary development designed to express Christianity's exclusive claim to truth. It may turn out that other faiths
have their own ways of making similar claims. It may be that,
like Francis Newman, we have an encounter with a wholly
different viewpoint which forces us to break out of a single
closed world and realize that there are in fact several possible
religious worlds.

People worry at this point, and say that when Europeans
ceased to believe that their own cultural assumptions were
absolute the long slide into scepticism and decline began. But
can we honestly wish to go back to Charlemagne's simple
certainties? Such 'simple faith was in fact nothing but pig-
headed ignorance and cruelty. Why not look for a compromise, if there is one?

## 3.4 *Time*

Following St Paul's lead, the early Christian Fathers developed a plan of universal history which held firm until the seventeenth century. It embedded the incarnation in a general view of the nature of Time and the course of history which now seems very strange to us, though it still seemed as obvious to Milton as to St Augustine over twelve centuries earlier.

*The span of universal history is very brief,* somewhere between 5000 and 7000 years. In antiquity there was already a common mythological belief in the destruction of the cosmos by fire every 5000 years or so. Christianity came on the scene with an Old Testament whose time-scale suggested that most of this period had already elapsed, and a New Testament which teaches that the End is nigh. It all fitted.

*Man is coeval with the world.* Genesis envisages no prehuman history. The visible creation had been made as a stage for man to walk on, and the animals for him to rule. Evil and suffering had spread through Nature only since the Fall of man.

*History is dispensational,* being arranged and organized by God in a series of theologically-distinct stages: Paradise, the patriarchs, the law and the gospel.

*The Golden Age is past.* Most traditional societies see the present era as one of decline, and Christianity found in the Bible elements which supported this point of view: the Paradise-myth, the longevity of the patriarchs, and even an apocalyptic version of the pagan sequence of gold, silver, bronze and iron ages (Daniel 2.32).

But how could the conservative view that the world has been getting worse ever since Eden be reconciled with the claim that we now live in the Age of Grace, the last and best period of all? It was done by saying two things:

First, *the incarnation is final.* The basic conditions of future human religious existence were unalterably laid down between the incarnation and the day of Pentecost. No further religious progress is possible during the years of Our Lord.

Secondly, *the best age of the church was the primitive period.* Ever since, the world has been getting older and more corrupt. Saints are fewer, faith grows weaker and Popes grow wickeder. There has to be a nadir of evil before the Last Day comes.

All these beliefs about time and history have passed away. We now measure the lifespan of the cosmos in billions of years, and it seems hard to think of it as nothing but a stage made for us, when we have arrived so late and live in so infinitesimal a corner of it. It is immoral to say that animals were made solely for our use and false to say that lions once lay down with lambs and will do so again. The old ideas of original righteousness, the Fall, and a series of dispensations seem plainly mythological. Above all, we no longer look to the past as a source of social norms for we are vividly aware of historical change.

Most Christians have now dispensed with the old beliefs about time that I have just described. But one of them is not easy to dispense with; for if God became incarnate once-for-all in Jesus then it does seem to follow that the incarnation stands over all subsequent centuries as an absolute that cannot be superseded but forever prescribes the form of human religious life. No amount of historical change – not even in a million years, if the human race survives that long – can diminish its authority one whit. It seems to follow that the faith, doctrines and morality of the New Testament will similarly always be intelligible, and always authoritative. The canon is closed, and nothing can be added to it.

Certainly many people think this, and certainly many Christian doctrines and forms of worship seem to be claiming a kind of historical immutability or timeless truth. But theologians are uneasy about such claims. They are very historically-minded, and have been so for a hundred years and more. They are uncomfortably aware of how the meanings of words and sentences inevitably change with the passage of time, and how very different Christianity has been in different periods. The belief that Christian faith is immutable from Pentecost to the End of history looks like an illusion, and a harmful one at that.

And with respect to the incarnation the question arises, 'History being what it is, how *can* there be a sequence of events, a life lived and a fact established in history which forever afterwards is absolute and unchangeable in its authority?'

## 3.5 *The limits of historical knowledge*

René Descartes (1596-1650), the founder of modern philosophy, was the man whose thinking and way of life typified the spirit of the new age of science. In his mature years he lived quietly in Holland. He ground lenses, and purchased carcasses from the butcher for dissection. He corresponded on matters of science and philosophy with the leading men of Europe, meditated and wrote his books. But he was not interested in learning and considered Latin and Greek a waste of time. He hardly ever read an old book. When a caller asked to see his library, Descartes showed him a partly-dissected calf, saying, 'Here are my books'.

For Descartes there were only two sources of knowledge that mattered. The first and most important was pure philosophical reasoning, the best way to truth of all, and the second was direct experiment and sense-observation. As for authority, tradition, scholarship and old books, he thought nothing of them. For him, the bookishness of the Renaissance and Reformation was over; it was a waste of time. Reason and sense-experience were sources of uncontaminated and immediate knowledge, but if you got involved with old books and history you were plunged into a morass of uncertainties and fruitless controversy.

In the Middle Ages people had taken a completely opposite

view. In a manuscript culture books were rare and precious and every author was an authority (*auctor, auctoritas*). The great systems of the schoolmen were harmonizations of the teachings of the received author-authorites. But at the Reformation the Protestants began a violent attack on the whole process by which church doctrine was elaborated and defended. Arguing that the church had added to and corrupted the original faith, the Protestants were beginning what we now call historical criticism. They succeeded in demonstrating that key documents to which Catholic apologists had long been in the habit of appealing were nothing but forgeries.

It was clear that the old practice of treating every ancient author as an authority was no longer good enough. If you wanted to cite a text in support of your views you first had to prove that it was genuine, and germane to the point at issue. Principles of historical criticism had to be worked out, and this was not easy to do. So for a long time history was a theological battleground, and the philosophers avoided it.

However, theologians cannot avoid the problem of history. Christianity has reached us by historical tradition (literally, 'handing-on'), and the church quotes historical evidence in support of the beliefs that it urges upon its members. For example, believers at the eucharist hear the words, ' . . . who, in the same night that he was betrayed, took bread; and, when he had given thanks, he broke it, and gave it to his disciples, saying, Take, eat, this is my Body which is given for you: Do this in remembrance of me . . .' Believers take this to imply that Jesus did live, did celebrate the Last Supper, did indeed speak these words, and meant by them what the church understands him to have meant. But the various New Testament accounts of the Last Supper are all different from each other, with a host of manuscript variations as well. Even the simple form of words over the bread is reported differently by Matthew, Mark, Luke and Paul, and not one of them has exactly the words I have just quoted fom the liturgy. And even if Jesus spoke some such words, there has not been general agreement among theologians or churches as to what he may have meant by them.

Now *at every single point and in every last detail the appeal to history ends in such uncertainties.* By the middle of the eighteenth century theologians had already recognized the problem. Rational historical judgment is indeed possible, but it can never yield anything more than a web of probabilities. Faith is supposed to be an unconditional assent to God's revealed truth; but if historical method is needed to discover it, we can never be certain what God's revealed truth actually *is*.

For 200 years theology has been haunted by this issue. It was stated very clearly by Isaac Berruyer, a French Jesuit, in his posthumously-published (and speedily Indexed) *Reflexions on faith*, 1762. Berruyer decided that we must give up the appeal to history, and put all the weight on the present teaching authority of the church:

> God has not willed that in the matter of belief the decisive reasoning of the Catholic should run thus:
> Jesus Christ has said in his Gospel, Take eat, this is my body.
> Therefore the Body of Jesus Christ is really present in the Eucharist.
> God has substituted for this way of reasoning another which is more adapted to meet all doubts: 'The Church of Jesus Christ teaches me that the Body of Jesus Christ is really present in the Eucharist: Therefore the words of Jesus Christ must be adequate to the meaning of the reality.'

Berruyer's line of argument leads to what was later to be called Catholic Modernism.

A Protestant who similarly wishes to overcome the uncertainty by appealing to authority will accept historical criticism of Catholic claims, but will refuse to permit criticism of the Bible. The Bible, he says, is God's revealed Word to men and must be read in a spirit of faith. 'I assert that it teaches the doctrines held in my group, and you must accept that.' But as everyone knows, different fundamentalist groups teach different doctrines.

G. E. Lessing (1729-1781) had an answer to this conservative Protestant position. After stating the general problem –
that there is no way of bridging the gap between the uncertainties of history and the supposed certainty of faith – he
considers an objector who says to him, 'You can be quite
sure, because the Gospel-writers were inspired and cannot be
mistaken.' Lessing replies, 'But the judgment that the
Gospel-writers were inspired and could not err is *itself* a
merely historical judgment. How can you prove it beyond
any possible doubt?'

So the rise of the critical historical method has been a major
challenge to traditional Christianity. The common response,
among both Catholics and Protestants, has been a heightened
appeal to authority, the authority of the church, tradition and
the Bible. But a number of courageous spirits have said, 'Let
us set aside questions of doctrine for the moment, and try
honestly to follow the critical historical method. Let us study
the New Testament and the development of Christianity as
rigorously as we can, and see where it leads us.' That is the
path taken by critical theologians but in the nature of the case
it does not and cannot lead to agreement. There is not now
and is never likely to be any generally-agreed picture of the
historical Jesus, and there is not now and is never likely to be
any generally-agreed explanation of the origins of the doctrine of the incarnation.

Modern knowledge is vast, but it is *in principle uncertain*.
This is true of both science and history. As you approach the
frontiers, in any subject, you enter a battlefield. Theology is
no exception. Nothing is certain: there are no expert-oracles.

A dilemma arises here, which every believer must face. In
1935 the psychologist R. H. Thouless showed in a classical
piece of research that people are much more sure they know
the answer to 'Are there angels in heaven?' than the answer
to 'Are there tigers in India?' He called this phenomenon *the
tendency to certainty in religious beliefs*. Indeed there is an inbuilt
desire for certainty in matters of faith, and until the seven-

teenth century theologians thought it was rationally justifi-able. Today, if you need that certainty, you will have to accept some authority in a non-rational way, because *proofs of the authority of Bible or church are themselves uncertain*. But if you follow the path of reason, you must give up the tradi-tional claim to certainty.

## 3.6 *Miracles and natural law*

Great and mysterious events take place in the world about us whose causes are not human, but which bear directly on human well-being. They include such things as the variations in the weather, the incidence of disease, the success or failure of the harvest, the occurrence of natural disasters, the motions of the heavenly bodies, and a host of minor ups and downs of fortune. The main area of overlap between religion and science lies in the fact that both of them have long been concerned with such events, simply because of the vital human importance of being able in some measure to under-stand, predict and control them.

In our science-based culture we have become used to regarding such events as produced by the regular operation of impersonal natural forces. But for most of its history Christ-ianity lived in a largely prescientific world in which it seemed natural to explain them in terms of the agency of invisible personal beings. To a considerable extent Christian doctrine and practice presupposed a supranaturalistic world-view, in which human life on earth is continually exposed to the influence of a good supernatural world above men, and an evil supernatural world below and within man. As late as 1662 the English *Book of Common Prayer* still diagnosed drought, famine and sickness in religious terms and pre-scribed forms of religious action for dealing with them.

It is not quite fair to say that religious thought had always been merely animistic. The Greeks had formulated the idea of an autonomous natural order in antiquity, and bequeathed it to Christians. Muslims regard the regular order of Nature as the expression of the sovereignty of God, and do not attach so much importance to mythological ideas of occasional divine intervention. But there is no doubt that mainstream Christian thought and practice was vividly mythological and indeed interventionist in its ideas about the manifestations of divine, angelic and demonic power in the world. Both in the external world and within their own hearts, people felt themselves to be continually experiencing temptations of the devil, attacks by evil spirits, tokens of divine favour and disfavour, warnings, judgments, graces and guidances.

In such a world miracles have a natural place. Small divine interventions – help in time of temptation, guidance in time of perplexity, answers to prayer, significant coincidences – were happening all the time. Miracles were more striking examples of the same thing, and the incarnation was the grandest case of the general principle of divine intervention to help and deliver man in time of need.

Now even before the scientific revolution Protestantism had begun to attack the most baroque excesses of medieval animism – things like the cult of saints, holy water, relics and exorcism. Catholics retorted that the divine authority of the church and God's approval of its doctrine and practice were proved by the present-day miracles being worked by the church's Saints. Nettled, the Protestants answered that these ecclesiastical miracles were frauds. The age of miracles is past: it ended with the death of the last Apostle.

I noticed a slight awkwardness at this point a few years ago, when I was involved in a public controversy about exorcism and had to look up what the classic Protestant and Anglican divines had said about the subject. There is no doubt that they detested the idea of Protestant ministers working miracles and casting out demons. But their distaste for these phenomena contrasts oddly with the New Testament's evident enthusiasm for them. They admitted that Jesus had been an exorcist and a miracle-worker, and they accepted that he had bequeathed the same powers to his followers. Why then were such things not to be done today? Were not the Catholics on stronger ground? If it is true that the Protestant view of man's relation to God is rational and moralistic in a way that excludes an animistic view of life, then sooner or later Protestants must ask questions about the gap between their own position and that of the New Testament.

At any rate, Protestant rationalism was an important forerunner of later and more secular forms of rationalism. The very effective Protestant critique of Catholic ecclesiastical miracles was to provide a splendid collection of good arguments for later freethinkers to borrow and use against the Bible and its belief in miracles, angels and demons.

During the seventeenth century men's attitude towards the external world was revolutionized. Instead of being explained in terms of the secret operation of spiritual powers and purposes, the world came to be seen in mechanical terms, and explained in terms of the uniform operation of mathematical laws of nature. Animism began to retreat rapidly. A classic example was the great comet whose appearance had for centuries been taken to portend political calamities. When Edmund Halley noticed its periodicity and successfully predicted its next appearance in 1758, his comet forever lost its old supernatural significance.

The decline of animism has been very slow and erratic, but it has happened. In my childhood the Sandman put children to sleep and Jack Frost made ice patterns on the windowpanes overnight, but I noticed the other day that my own children had not heard of them and had felt no need of them. Innumerable small superstitions to do with magpies and ladybirds, mirrors and ladders, beginnings and endings, salt and blood are fading away. The 'supernatural', in the newspaper sense, is now a silly-season joke, and the preoccupation of eccentrics. There is a noticeable shift of emphasis away from the grosser kinds of intercessory prayer towards meditation, and where intercessory prayer is practised it seems to have partly an expressive function, and partly the function of 'raising the consciousness' of the congregation.

The more the natural order appears to be autonomous and law-abiding, the more miracles are isolated. They are no longer vivid illustrations of a general principle, but startlingly dramatic exceptions to the general course of things. They become at once harder to believe and (if true) more significant.

But as miracles become steadily fewer and more isolated, the strain gets greater. Few people today would try to defend the Old Testament miracles, but they might hope to keep the gospel miracles. But the critics say that the miracle-stories in the gospels can be sufficiently explained in terms of traditional symbolism, standard techniques for developing stories, the culture of the period, and the theological purposes of the gospel writers. The question of historicity does not arise, and even if it did, could not be answered with confidence.

A danger of circularity arises at this point. Some people say, 'I believe the miracles because of the incarnation. If Jesus is God incarnate, he may have had powers unique in the whole of human history.' But if you believe the miracles because of the incarnation you cannot also say that you believe the incarnation because of the miracles. And in any case is there not something very odd about a miracle-working incarnate God with powers no human being in all history has had? Why did he heal some and not others, right some wrongs and not all wrongs? What picture of God does this imply?

Today the critics have largely surrendered the gospel miracles. Now the incarnation is left in complete isolation, the one remaining example of an idea of supernatural intervention in the world which was once all-pervasive. It has lost the context of daily experience and belief which formerly made it credible and intelligible.

## 3.7 *Moral criticisms*

In 3.1 I sketched the traditional Christian history of salvation and said ironically that if someone really claims to be an orthodox traditional believer, then that must be what he believes. In fact, of course, nobody today believes the entire story exactly as Augustine or Milton tell it. As we have seen, it has been shattered by huge changes in our world-picture, our knowledge of other cultures, our conception of Time, and our understanding of history and nature.

In addition, it is also morally objectionable. It is now hard to imagine, and even harder to relish the thought of, a world in which my very thoughts are not my own but are troop-movements in a war between supernatural powers. All my good thoughts are implanted by God, all my bad ones by Satan. My soul is a battlefield over which they rage back and forth in their endless struggle for supremacy.

Equally uninviting is the conception of divine justice built into the traditional story. It seems inexplicable that the whole human race should be born in a condition that merits eternal damnation, merely because of a sin committed at the beginning of time by our primal ancestors; and very odd that the punishment of an innocent should so abruptly change God's mind that his forgiveness is now poured out as generously as his wrath was before. To say that the punishment has in some sense been borne by God himself is even more confusing. Does God punish himself for his own mismanagement? And everybody is perplexed by the dualism which requires that every human being be eventually allotted either the greatest conceivable reward or the greatest conceivable punishment.

In addition, the incarnation-doctrine has been attacked as having at least some connection with absolutist, intolerant and persecuting elements in the Christian tradition. The old charge that the Jews were guilty of 'deicide' is an example: they rejected their own God when he came in person to them, so they must be the most accursed of all peoples.

Christianity is seen, not so much as the fulfilment of Judaism,
but rather as a new faith based on God's rejection of the Jews.
Again, any monotheistic faith which believes in one final
revelation believes itself to be in possession of one absolute
truth, and so has no incentive to respect diversity of opinion.
When it is further claimed that the One God has once and for
all embodied himself in human form and in that human form
has transmitted his own plenary authority to his church,
surely the tendency to absolutism and intolerance must be all
the stronger? Religious doctrines are seldom really rigorously
connected with each other, but (in an informal way) is it not
true that the doctrine of the incarnation leads to the doctrines
of the church's indefectibility and infallibility, to the maxim
that 'outside the church there is no salvation', and so to un-
limited claims for the church's authority? In the past, the case
was certainly argued in just that way. As Boniface VIII put it
in the Bull *Unam Sanctam* of 1302, the church's authority,

> ... although given to man and exercized by man, is not human
> but rather Divine, being given to Peter at God's mouth and founded
> for him and his successors on a rock ... Whoever, therefore, resists
> this power thus ordained by God, resists the ordinance of God ...
> Consequently we declare, state, define and pronounce that it is
> altogether necessary for salvation to every human creature to be
> subject to the Roman Pontiff. [7]

Modern theologians who defend the incarnation are very
much aware of these various objections, and give revised
accounts which they claim are free of the old associations.
They present the incarnation as witnessing to supremely
important and precious religious and moral values. In the
incarnation God has humbled himself out of pure love and
shared the human condition. God has taken the initiative in
crossing the gulf between God and man, so that our approach
to God has been made possible by God himself. The incarnate Lord Jesus Christ is a bridge to God built for us by God.

Furthermore, the incarnation reveals that God's own
nature is loving and personal. God is not a bare, transcendent

Monad (i.e., a wholly undifferentiated abstract unity), for there is an eternal loving communion of persons within God. In the incarnation the eternal communion of the Father and the Son is translated into human terms in the shape of the human faith of Jesus. His exaltation into God is the basis and prototype of a general taking-up of the human into God. In Christ God is seen at our side, sharing and experiencing the world's evil and suffering, yet triumphing by the power of love and exalting the human into eternity.

On this account the incarnation is central to a deeply personal, moral and even humanist vision of God and man's redemption. Human destiny is an eternal personal loving communion with God in and through the humanity of God in Jesus. Those who present the incarnation in these terms would certainly repudiate the cruel and savage elements in the traditional story of salvation. They reject the idea of an arbitrary and incomprehensible divine justice, and cannot fairly be charged with wishing to see the return of an intolerant and theocratic social order. As they would say, true theocracy is not a reign of power and worldly authority but of humble and suffering love.

One of my difficulties with this modern incarnational theology is that, in order to keep the doctrine without the unpleasant corollaries that were drawn in the past, it says very peculiar things about God. Refusing to portray God as an absolute Monarch, it flies to the opposite extreme and portrays God as human, humbling himself, experiencing suffering and change, and incorporating humanist personal values into the divine being. The resulting religion, with its rhetoric of humanized divinity and divinized humanity, seems to me to be a wish-fulfilment, a projection which is neither truly religious nor truly nourishing to the soul. The old authoritarian feudal theology and the new romantic humanist theology seem both to be very remote from the prophetic faith which is the true core of biblical religion and was the religion of Jesus himself.

# 4

## The Impact of Biblical Criticism

### 4.1 *Scriptural infallibility*

Like other scriptural religions, Christianity traditionally regarded its holy book as somehow coming from God and possessing divine authority; but for many centuries the idea was not seriously challenged from within and so was not exactly defined. Only when the Reformation raised questions about authority in matters of faith were the churches forced to work out their views about the nature of biblical inspiration.

As usual, the Roman Catholic position is as clear and strict as any. On 8 April 1546 the Council of Trent described God as the 'author' of both the Old and New Testaments and said that the apostolic writings in the New Testament were produced 'at the *dictation* of the Holy Spirit'. On 24 April 1870 the Vatican Council declared that the biblical books are not merely free from errors, but were written by the *prompting* of the Holy Spirit and so have God for their author. Finally, on 18 November 1965 the Second Vatican Council declared that the biblical books, having been written under the *inspiration* of the Holy Spirit, have God for their author. They teach 'firmly, faithfully and without error that truth which God wanted put into the sacred writings for the sake of our salvation'.

I have italicized *dictation, prompting* and *inspiration* to draw attention to a certain doctrinal shift. The sense in which God is the author of the Bible has become a little less direct, and Vatican II limits scripture's inerrancy to what it teaches for the sake of our salvation. It is no longer claimed that scripture is inerrant on such matters as astronomy. But Vatican II still says God is the author of the Bible, and draws the classic parallel:

> For the words of God, expressed in human language, have been made like human discourse, just as of old the Word of the eternal Father, when he took to himself the weak flesh of humanity, became like other men. . . .[8]

This analogy between 'the Word of God written' and 'the Word of God incarnate' goes back to the early Fathers and is appealed to by both sides in the controversy about the incarnation. The conservatives say that just as Jesus is fully human and yet also truly divine, so scripture is written by men and in human language and yet is also the Word of God. The revisionists say that just as we have been obliged to give up the idea that the Bible is a book 'literally' written by God through human instruments, so we must also give up the idea of a 'literal' incarnation of God in the man Jesus. We may still speak of the Bible as a supremely important religious book and we may still claim that 'God was in Christ' in a special way. But the old hard-edged objectivity has to be given up, because of the culturally-conditioned and historical character of language in the first case and of human existence in the second.

Vatican II recognizes this last point. In the text quoted above, the Dogmatic Constitution *On Divine Revelation,* it says that the biblical books were written by men who had purposes of their own in writing, purposes which were human and distinct from the divine purpose of which they were the vehicles:

> . . . the interpreter of sacred Scripture, in order to see clearly what God wanted to communicate to us, should carefully investigate what meaning the sacred writers really intended, and what God wanted to manifest by means of their words.

This task of finding out what the sacred writers meant requires scholarship, because the Bible is not written in the form of oracles addressed by God in direct speech *(oratio recta)* to human readers in general. On the contrary, it is very complex and indirect. The interpreter of the Bible, therefore,

> ... must, among other things, have regard for 'literary forms.' For truth is proposed and expressed in a variety of ways, depending on whether a text is history of one kind or another, or whether its form is that of prophecy, poetry, or some other type of speech. The interpreter must investigate what meaning the sacred writer intended to express and actually expressed in particular circumstances as he used contemporary literary forms in accordance with the situation of his own time and culture. For the correct understanding of what the sacred writer wanted to assert, due attention must be paid to the customary and characteristic styles of *perceiving* [my italics – D.C.] speaking, and narrating which prevailed at the time of the sacred writer, and to the customs men normally followed at that period in their everyday dealings with one another.

This passage shows how far Christian thought has moved since the sixteenth-century days when God merely dictated the text of the Bible to human secretaries. In fact it has moved so far that there scarcely remains any sense in which God *clearly* speaks to the ordinary reader through the pages of the Bible. Where an old text is concerned it is often difficult to divine the author's intention with any confidence: consider, for example, the ambiguities of trying to infer Shakespeare's own beliefs from his plays. In the case of a biblical book, there are often textual uncertainties as a result of centuries of manuscript transmission; there are often difficulties of translation; and in many cases the book is highly composite and has no single clear message, or has been re-edited by someone who has modified its original message. There is no single clear answer to the question, 'What did the author of the book of Job intend to say about the problem of evil?'

But this is only the beginning of the difficulties. We are supposed to discover the author's intention, and then go behind that to discover God's intention. The two may be very different, for after all Christians hold that three-fourths of the Bible (the Old Testament) is partly obsolete, *even though* it has

God for its author. What is more, very different doctrines are taught in different biblical books. We are not even quite sure which books are biblical, for different churches reckon different books canonical. There are ancient oriental churches whose New Testament canon is somewhat different from the one we are used to.

In view of all these puzzles, and many more, the sense in which God is the author of the Bible has become very attenuated. What can be meant by saying that in all these very discordant human voices we hear, clearly and unmistakably, one divine voice? Vatican II meets the difficulty by saying that the church is the true interpreter of scripture:

> ... sacred tradition, sacred Scripture, and the teaching authority of the Church, in accord with God's most wise design, are so linked and joined together that one cannot stand without the others...

So the text and canon are what the church says they are and mean what the church says they mean, and Vatican II is left asserting two things which do not really cohere. On the one hand technical critical scholarship is necessary in order to discover what the biblical writings mean, and the nature of scholarship is such that its conclusions will always be uncertain and controversial. On the other hand it is also asserted that God is the author of the Bible, and the church is divinely guided to make correct judgments about what God is saying through the Bible. Two utterly different views about the nature of religious truth and how we can get hold of it are held in uneasy coexistence.

However, in spite of this continuing uncertainty, and the tension between church authority and the theologians that it produces, the important thing is that a change has taken place in the way we see both the Bible and the incarnation. Jesus was a man of his time, as people say, and the Bible is a book that belongs to a certain time. The fact of profound historical change between the biblical period and the present day is now recognized, and even the strictest fundamentalist does not think of the Holy Book quite as people once did.

It is now difficult to imagine the views once held by Jews, Christians and Muslims. It was thought that God had composed the Torah (the five Books of Moses) in heaven. Hebrew was God's own language, taught by him to our first parents in paradise, and the ancestor of all other natural languages. God had created the world by speaking Hebrew words, and a kabbalist might hope to discover the combinations of Hebrew consonants by which he could himself become a creator-magician: hence the legend of the Golem, the artificial man created by Rabbi Judah Loew ben Bezabel. Such impieties apart, the Holy Book contained all truth, not just religious truth. Its study was life's greatest joy, and its richness of meaning inexhaustible. No other learning was necessary, and there could not be any secular literature unrelated to it.

In Orthodox Judaism, especially in Eastern Europe, something of the old strength of faith in the Holy Book survived till very recently. The beauty of it, the pain of its loss, and the sad inevitability of that loss, have been described very finely by a number of Jewish novelists – S. Y. Agnon, Isaac Bashevis Singer, Chaim Potok. In Christianity the nearest parallel, perhaps, is a book like Edmund Gosse's *Father and Son* (1907), which describes the traumatic effect of Darwinism on Philip Gosse, a Plymouth Brother and zoologist. We have not yet fully understood the huge change in religious outlook which has to follow the loss of the old certainties.

## 4.2 *The supernatural apparatus and the question of myth*

Like many people who have been trained mainly in natural science and philosophy, I used to be somewhat disdainful of biblical critics. I thought they were not real religious thinkers, but mere scribes, commenting on commentaries and building houses of cards. But this attitude was mistaken. Modern biblical criticism is one of the most highly technically-refined of all arts subjects and its achievements have been remarkable.

Its history goes back a long way. Between 1500 and 1700 Western society gradually changed from being tradition-directed to being critical and progressive. The two main stimuli were the Protestant Reformation and the rise of modern science.

In a tradition-directed society the main intellectual effort is put into maintaining the received tradition intact. You may systematize, develop and add to tradition, but you cannot prune it back because you cannot risk losing anything. It is assumed that the whole body of received tradition is a perfect unity, so that any contradictions in it must be merely apparent. If you notice a contradiction you do not think of eliminating one branch of it: on the contrary, you immediately seek some way of resolving it by further doctrinal elaboration. For example, tradition says that Moses wrote the Torah, or Pentateuch. But the Torah contains accounts of many matters that Moses surely could not have known about, such as Moses' own funeral. Does this falsify the traditional doctrine that Moses wrote the Torah? Certainly not. Tradition also says that Moses was a prophet, so we have only to postulate that God granted Moses supernatural knowledge of things that he could not have known about by himself. When you are in the habit of appealing to mystery, to sacred authority and to supernatural power you can get yourself out of almost any difficulty and answer almost any objection.

Protestantism and printing broke these ways of thinking. Protestantism said that the modern church was different from the early church, and the doctrines of the modern church were different from those taught in the New Testament. It shattered the unity of tradition and forced people to think about historical change and ask what the New Testament actually does say. It was one thing to hear the New Testament sung in Latin on Sundays; it was a very different thing to read it in Greek or a modern vernacular in one's own home on a weekday. And the question of what the New Testament really says became all the more urgent as rival schools of thought developed among the Protestants themselves.

The rise of modern natural science was equally influential. Between 1600 and 1700 the leading thinkers gradually came to believe that all events in the physical world happen in accordance with universal laws of nature. Appeal to occult spiritual agency, to miracles and the supernatural, began to look less and less plausible. One very good reason for becoming interested in biblical criticism is that when we read Exodus or Matthew we react with astonishment and incredulity. The world is not like that: things do not happen that way. How is this book to be explained?

A good early example of how the questions arose and how a great mind tackled them is to be found in the *Theological-Political Treatise* of Baruch Spinoza (1632-77), the Amsterdam lens-grinder, heretical Jew and philosopher.

Spinoza was convinced that everything in nature happens according to universal laws which proceed from the wisdom of God. Popular opinion sees the hand of God in the inexplicable and the prodigious but, says Spinoza, this attitude is the very reverse of the truth. If a miracle is an inexplicable prodigy then by definition it cannot tell us anything about God. On the contrary, if a miracle happened it would tell *against* belief in God, for it would be a hiatus in the God-maintained order of the world. So Spinoza is convinced that miracles cannot happen and have not happened, and that he can give natural explanations of the biblical miracles and the formation of the miracle-stories. He quotes the example of the battle of Joshua against the five kings (Joshua 10), when the sun stood still in heaven to give the Israelites time to complete their victory over their enemies. What actually happened, says Spinoza, was that daylight lasted longer than usual. That is a pretty commonplace suggestion, but what is more striking is Spinoza's explanation of why the story is told as it is. He makes a series of observations. He says that the language of scripture is poetic, being addressed to the imagination and the will of people at large rather than to the understanding of philosophers. It tends to emphasize God's immediate control over events and may omit to mention that God acts through natural causes. Secondly, Spinoza points out that people very rarely give purely empirical descriptions of events. The way we describe events important to us is moulded by our beliefs and our interests. The ancient Israelites believed that the earth was at rest and the sun moved daily over it. They wanted to say that God was on their side and that the sun was not a pagan deity but a creature subject to God's will. For all these reasons, they related after the battle that God had arrested the sun to give them the victory.

In many respects Spinoza's ideas are rather dated, but even after 300 years he is still very acute. The modern reader finds the miraculous and supernatural apparatus of the Bible a problem. Spinoza says it is a mistake to take it literally. It is generated by a combination of factors – the literary forms of the Bible, which are often closer to poetry than to modern science and philosophy, the different cosmological beliefs held in former times, and the strong religious interests that have shaped the writing.

Where factors of these three kinds are involved modern theologians use the word 'myth'. Spinoza doesn't, for, as Professor Maurice Wiles pointed out in his discussion of 'Myth in Theology' in the eighth essay in *The Myth of God Incarnate*, the word 'myth' only came into common use in the early nineteenth century. But Spinoza's concerns are close to those of modern theologians, and he is sometimes called the founder of biblical criticism. For him as for us, what may broadly be called the scientific view of the world is so dominant that all typically prescientific ways of explaining things have come to seem puzzling. The term 'myth' is nowadays used as a sort of holdall into which all the problems are packed.

Myth crept into theology gradually. The German philologist C. G. Heyne (1729-1812) introduced the word (*muthos* is Greek for 'story') in connection with classical literature. Myth is the most primitive form of poetry, found among all peoples in their earliest beginnings. In the form of *saga*, it may have a historical basis. Other myths telling of the birth of the gods and the establishment of the cosmos have explanatory and ethical functions.

J. G. Eichhorn (1752-1827) applied these ideas to the Old Testament, arguing that there could be no reason for discriminating between Greek and Jewish mythology.

But could the term be applied to the gospels? After all, the gospels are not set in prehistoric time and do not deal with legendary ancestor-figures. They are set firmly in recorded history. If ideas of myth and folktale were to be applied to the gospels, one needed firm criteria for distinguishing history from myth and for explaining how the accounts of Jesus and his deeds have become mythologized. J. P. Gabler (1753-1826) pointed out that at the time of Jesus people did not distinguish between the facts and the conceptual apparatus in which they clothed the facts when describing them, a distinction of which Kant's philosophy had recently made people aware. Thus Gabler writes: 'At the time of Jesus angels belonged to *the theological machinery of the Jews* ... God worked everywhere through angels ... every incomprehensible event, every unexpected sudden help must have been the work of an angel... *Where we think of an indirect providence of God, the Jews thought of angels*.'[9]

That instructive quotation shows the modern awareness of cultural relativity. What Gabler is really saying is, 'Don't think of angels as real beings. Think of them as human cultural products. Angels are not things out there in the world, but human conceptions in terms of which, at one time, people used to explain events. Angels belong to the history of ideas, and *not* to the furniture of the universe.'

The most brilliant and thoroughgoing analysis of the gospels from the mythical point of view was *The Life of Jesus*

*Critically Examined* by D. F. Strauss (1808-1874), published in 1835-6. The English translation by George Eliot appeared in 1846.

Strauss aimed to prove that the mythical interpretation of the gospels was the true one, and he set out to demolish both the supernaturalists who read the gospels literally and the rationalists who gave naively reductive explanations. He recognized the importance of eschatological fervour to Jesus and his first followers. It had supplied the motive for mythicizing Jesus, and the Old Testament and later Jewish tradition had supplied the symbolic materials. Strauss recognized that the gospel of John was almost useless as an historical source, a very important point because orthodox belief in the incarnation rests mainly upon John. In the other (synoptic) gospels myth was most evident in the accounts of Jesus' birth, his relations with the Baptist, his miracles, his transfiguration, his detailed predictions about his passion, and the whole passion story from Jesus' entry into Jerusalem through to his resurrection and ascension. On the other hand, Strauss was convinced that Jesus had lived, had been a follower of the Baptist, had delivered in Galilee much of the teaching ascribed to him by the synoptic writers, had believed himself to be the Messiah, had gone to Jerusalem expecting rejection and hoping for God's vindication, and had been arrested, tried and crucified. So although Strauss had eliminated the supernatural apparatus of the gospels as mythical, he ended with a portrait of Jesus which is rather conservative by modern standards.

The violent attacks on the book finished Strauss' career, but the book itself could not be put down. It remains the first great work of modern theology and the word 'myth' is still a red rag to a bull. The reason is, now as then, that to explain the supernatural apparatus of the gospels as 'mythological' is in effect to explain it naturalistically – that is, as a human cultural product rather than a divine revelation. When we are told that such-and-such an idea is mythological we are being told not to worry, for that is how people used to think, but we do not think like that now.

Theologians like to say that there is a very big difference between the popular sense of myth (as a falsehood) and the theological use of myth to mean stories about the actions of supernatural beings and their dealings with men. But maybe the difference is not so very great. Commenting on a story like that of the temptation of Jesus by the Devil in the wilderness, the modern critic will say that given the beliefs of the time, the conceptual resources available, and the things the writer wanted to say about Jesus, he naturally told that story in that way. It can all be explained, it all makes sense. The plain man replies, 'Did it actually happen, and is there a Devil?' The critic will reply, 'No, of course not.' The plain man will then say, 'So it isn't true, then?' To the plain man modern biblical criticism looks sceptical, or at any rate rather too clever for its own good. The controversies about the word 'myth' which have flared up from time to time since are explosions of irritation, and perhaps of anxiety that theology is becoming more sceptical than it openly admits.

But there is a reply to the plain man. His pose of bluff take-it-literally commonsense is a fraud. The thing to say to him is, 'You know very well that there is no Devil, there are no angels, physical miracles do not happen, and ideas of special divine intervention are childish. So don't pretend otherwise. In the Bible itself the supernatural apparatus is strongest in folk tradition (Elijah, Elisha, the synoptic gospels), in apocalyptic symbolism, and in liturgical praise for redemption. The more sophisticated biblical writers have surprisingly little need of it.'

## 4.3 *The human Jesus*

Modern biblical critics are mainly interested in the beliefs of the early Christian writers, and are cagey about historicity. A good deal can be said about what Matthew thought of Jesus, whereas only a little can be said about what Jesus was really like. But, broadly speaking, Strauss in 1835 was already on the right lines. Though he himself had second thoughts about St John's gospel, his early view of it was endorsed and established by F. C. Baur in 1847. John is relatively late and unhistorical.

Some people still dispute this, and may cite as authorities the names of two twentieth-century British writers, William Temple and C. H. Dodd. But Temple's *Readings in St John's Gospel* (1939–40),[10] whatever its merits or demerits as a work of devotion, is of no value as a work of historical criticism; and Dodd in his *Historical Tradition in the Fourth Gospel* (1963)[11] was only arguing that St John preserves some early traditions. He did not argue, and no one can plausibly argue, that the historical Jesus spoke the discourses that John puts on his lips.

Because of the importance of the question, there have been repeated attempts to defend the historicity of John. F. C. Baur certainly dated John far too late, and nowadays it is argued that the gospel is early in date, that its historical framework for Jesus' life rests on good early tradition, and that there are many primitive elements in its doctrine. All this may possibly be true, but it does not touch the central question: could Jesus have thought and spoken of himself in the way represented in the great Johannine discourses? The answer is still, No.

The position is that in the synoptic gospels (Matthew, Mark and Luke), once we strip off a fairly thin varnish of editing and early Christian belief, a clear portrait emerges of a first-century Jewish teacher who fits well into his historical context. His acts, his ways of speaking and the things he said can all be paralleled. He is historically convincing, whereas John's very different Jesus is totally unconvincing. John's Jesus is a supernatural figure who has come down from heaven to earth. He is fully apprised of his own exalted status and teaches it openly. He *remembers* living with God in eternity! His task is to proclaim himself as God's Son, the bridge between earth and heaven, the light of the world and bread of life.

Now the historical Jesus cannot have been both like the Jesus of John and the Jesus of the synoptics. The gulf is far too wide. And if he had really been as John describes him, how on earth can we explain the origin of the synoptic gospels? Why should those writers have suppressed the overwhelming and extraordinary teaching about his own status that John's Jesus gives? The only plausible view is that the real Jesus was much more like the Jesus of the synoptics and that John's Jesus developed later. With hindsight John projects back into Jesus' lifetime the beliefs about Jesus current in John's own circle two or three generations after Jesus' death, and claims that the historical Jesus had presented himself as he appeared to be to some Christians of the 90s – a heavenly, perhaps even divine, figure.

So for over a century it has been common ground among biblical critics that the historical Jesus must be seen as a human figure firmly embedded in a particular and rather strange historical context; and there has been a parallel emphasis on the humanity of Christ in theology. It is generally agreed that it is important to resist 'docetism', the view that Jesus was not truly human but merely a manifestation of a divine being in a temporary human guise.

Docetism appeared in very early times. Some lines in the New Testament are perhaps directed against it (for example I John 4. 1-3; II John 7). It can be seen in the apocryphal gospels, which contain some repulsive stories: the infant Jesus rides on a sunbeam, turns toy animals into real ones, strikes dead a playmate who accidentally bumps into him, and laughs at the suggestion that he (who is omniscient) needs to go to school. One is not surprised to read that Joseph took him by the ear; but, for reasons that Freud has described, fantasies of omnipotent saviour-figures have a perennial appeal all over the world. They still appear in comic books, in science fiction, and in popular thrillers. Jesus has in the past all too often been seen as such a figure, and theologians are agreed in wanting to be rid of docetism for good and all.

But the war against docetic fantasies, carried to its logical conclusion, suggests that John's Jesus is docetic and even that the doctrine of the incarnation itself is docetic. Most agree that Jesus was a man and did not have a secret identity and supernatural powers that he could call upon at will. But if it is suggested that the obvious inference is that the classical doctrine of his divinity must therefore now be abandoned, then agreement ends and controversy begins.

## 4.4 *The apocalyptic Jesus*

Strauss was also right in seeing the importance of eschatology to Jesus, and the leading gospel critics since his day have emphasized the idea still more strongly. Johannes Weiss (*Jesus' Proclamation of the Kingdom of God*, 1892) and Albert Schweitzer (*The Mystery of the Kingdom of God*, 1901) held that Jesus' entire outlook and message were governed by the expectation of the coming of the Kingdom of God within a generation. The greatest twentieth-century gospel critic, Rudolf Bultmann (1884-1976) took the same view.

There is considerable disagreement in detail. According to Strauss Jesus believed himself to be the Messiah and may at first have hoped to sweep straight to his messianic glory without having to die. But he came to recognize that his suffering and death were part of his messianic destiny and went to Jerusalem to meet his ordeal in the hope that after his death he would return on the clouds of heaven as the glorious Son of Man. The present age of world-history would end and the final reign of God would begin.

Johannes Weiss (1863-1914) thought that Jesus did not regard himself as being yet either Messiah or Son of Man. During the present age the cosmos is divided into two zones: earth under the dominion of Satan, and heaven, where God is King. Here on earth Jesus and his disciples struggle against Satan and pray for the coming of God's Kingdom to earth. But there is nothing Jesus can do to expedite the coming of the Kingdom. The only difference between Jesus and the Baptist is that Jesus hopes that when the Kingdom does come he himself will be appointed Messiah (or Christ) and Son of Man.

Today it is widely thought that Jesus did not claim any messianic titles for himself. It is very noticeable that nowhere in the gospels is he portrayed as publicly proclaiming his own messiahship as part of his message. He merely lets out or admits the secret of it on two or three more or less private occasions. Among the scholars there is a wide variety of views as to whether there was some sense in which the Kingdom was already present in Jesus' ministry, when its full consummation was expected, whether Jesus identified himself with the coming Son of Man and so on. The best explanation of this diversity is that the gospels themselves are inconsistent, because eschatological beliefs are always complex, symbolic and not wholly coherent. But there is no doubt about the general point that Jesus' words and deeds were deeply influenced by very strange eschatological ideas.

In the earliest surviving Christian writing we hear of anxiety that some believers are dying before the End has come. This was apparently a shock, for it had been expected that believers would not die (I Thessalonians 4. 13-18). In Mark (9.1) Jesus is represented as slightly modifying that expectation: 'There are some standing here who will not taste death before they see the kingdom of God come with power.' Much later, in II Peter 3.4 we hear of scoffers who say 'Where is the promise of his coming?', why is nothing changing, why is the world just as it has always been? These passages and many others (e.g., Matthew 10.23; I Corinthians 7. 29, 31; 10. 11; Romans 13.11) point irresistibly to the conclusion that the Baptist, Jesus, and Jesus' first followers expected the End very soon. Jesus may not have clearly envisaged any time at

all between his own death and the arrival of the Son of Man –
whether or not that figure was to be himself. The first believers expected not to die, or at any rate not all to die. The last
flicker of this belief was the medieval legend, based on John
21. 22f., that St John lingered on, over a thousand years old,
in a remote Middle-Eastern monastery waiting for his Lord's
coming.

In this primitive eschatological faith the idea of the incarnation played no part. Its place was taken by the idea of the Son
of Man or the Messiah as eschatological deliverer. But as time
went by incarnational Christianity slowly developed to take
its place. The incarnation belongs in the context of a whole
circle of ideas quite different from the earliest faith. In incarnational Christianity the present world-order is regarded as
more-or-less permanent, and Jesus' sojourn in heaven
whence he reigns invisibly over the church is also regarded as
more-or-less permanent. The incarnation sanctifies this
world, and establishes the church as a permanent historical
institution, the bridge between earth and heaven. With the
incarnation go the ideas of the santification of human flesh
through the sacraments, an organized universal church, and
life as a pilgrimage towards heaven.

Now if all this is true, developed gentile Christianity of the
sort which was beginning to take shape towards the end of
the first century has very little to do with Jesus or the faith of
the first generation. It is a new religion developed to replace
the original faith.

So the importance of eschatology to Jesus and the first
Christians poses some very awkward questions to orthodox
believers. There are various possible solutions. We may conclude that the Jehovah's Witnesses are the group which is
today nearest to New Testament Christianity. A second possible view is that, though some early Christians obviously
were apocalyptically-minded, Jesus himself was not. Early
Christian apocalypticism has been projected back upon him
in the gospels. A third theory is that Jesus is 'himself the

Kingdom': his message was that it had already come, being secretly present in his own person and deeds. Along these lines one might try to reconcile the primitive eschatology with the later incarnational belief. There are various possible theories: but the problem must be faced. Too often it is quietly ignored.


### 4.5 *The inaccessible Jesus*

In about the year 160 the early Christian writer Tatian produced the first 'Harmony' of the gospels, a life of Christ written by conflating or interweaving the contents of all four gospels. It was long a popular book. If the gospels are wholly historically true and can be woven together in that way, then Christians are in possession of a rich and detailed portrait of Jesus.

By contrast, the critical view of Jesus always seems very meagre to people who encounter it for the first time. Strauss, Schweitzer and Bultmann were all thought sceptics. It was a shock to realize that not a single line from the gospels can be taken as certainly historically reliable. Every detail must be weighed, and the portrait of Jesus that emerges is a mere web of conjectures. Because ancient man did not have an inner life in the post-renaissance sense, and the texts supply no real data about it, Jesus' psychology or 'personality' is an enigma and must remain so. All we can guess is that he was a very strange character who appeared crazed even to some of his contemporaries. He could fascinate, astonish or repel. It is generally agreed that he was a Galilean Jew who lived between about $-10$ and $+30$CE, that he was a follower of the Baptist, that he travelled about Palestine and especially within Galilee, that he spoke in parables about the Kingdom of God and that he was crucified in Jerusalem.

That is about the sum of what we can say with a high degree of confidence about Jesus. In addition I for one claim that by analysis of the linguistic forms of the teaching credited

to him in the synoptic gospels we can grasp the most important features of his religious message.

At the next level down, we can with a fair degree of
confidence say a good deal more about the kind of man he
was, the kinds of activity he engaged in, the themes of his
message and the circumstances of his death. But there are
two limits to this enterprise. The first is that the order of
events in the gospels has been determined by the evangelists.
They received only a very broad outline and a large number
of small individual anecdotes, and the order in which they
have arranged them is their own. They differ among themselves in their decisions about where to place particular anecdotes. So there is no hope of being able to trace any development in Jesus' message or strategy. Secondly, the anecdotes
themselves fall into set linguistic forms which have clearly
been created by the process of handing on by word of mouth.
In such a case a very small one-line historical nugget gets
elaborated into a good story, and maybe an illuminating
story, but historically there is only the nugget.

Anecdotes about the sayings of great men which are passed
down by oral tradition still have that quality. I remember
hearing that Churchill, on hearing of the illness of the
austerely puritanical Labour politician Stafford Cripps, said
slowly and very seriously, 'Nothing trivial, I hope?' I also
remember hearing that a nervous journalist sent to interview
De Gaulle could think of nothing better to say than that it was
a very nice day, whereupon the great man leaned over him
and murmured confidentially, 'Thank you'. If I were to relate
these stories to amuse an audience I would elaborate them
(indeed, I have done so) in order to heighten the effect of the
punchline. Every comedian knows or ought to know that
there are rules for developing a story so that it makes its best
impact. But the stories I have just told, though doubtless
amusing and maybe true to the characters of the notables
concerned, have as people say 'lost nothing in the telling'.
The historical nucleus around which they have been

developed is only a one-liner, a single undated glimpse.

The anecdotes about Jesus arose in a culture where memory was not refreshed by print and in a community in an intense and exalted state of religious excitement. They have been developed with a view to maximizing their religious impact. Their historical nucleus is little more than a one-liner, and it is usually very hard to assess. We have to conclude that lives of Christ are efforts to make a loaf out of a few crumbs. The question is bound to arise, 'Do we know enough about Jesus to justify *any* doctrine of Christ at all?'

It can fairly be pointed out that the documents about Jesus are closer to the founder, and have emerged from a better-known historical setting, than is the case with any other ancient religion. The Buddha, Moses, Confucius and Lao-Tse are historically quite inaccessible. Muhammad is the nearest analogy to the case of Jesus, but early seventh-century Arabia is pretty obscure territory and the traditions about Muhammad's life had plenty of time to develop before being written down a century after the Prophet's death. First-century Palestine, by contrast, is very well known and both literary and archaeological evidence is abundant. Once we have adjusted ourselves to the critical view of Jesus we may realize that he is after all pretty solidly rooted in known history and we do know something about him, even if not much.

Nevertheless, the fact remains that our knowledge of Jesus is not great, and is in principle no more than probable. How can something so serious as religious commitment be based on such shaky foundations?

One popular reply is that though our independent critical-historical knowledge of Jesus is slight, we do have many documents of early Christian faith. It is sufficient to believe the apostolic faith by trusting the early Christian verdict upon him. There are many voices, and they speak loud and clear.

This answer would be more convincing if, from the first, Christians had unanimously taken one consistent view of

Jesus which is continuous with Jesus' own message and view of himself. But they have not. As we have seen, we know just enough about Jesus to see that there is a puzzling jump between him and every form of Christianity. New Testament verdicts upon Jesus are already varied, and there has been considerable development since. It is highly doubtful whether there is a single New Testament theology, and if there is, whether any body of Christians now believes it.

So I suspect we come to a parting of the ways. There are in the end two possibilities, neither of them orthodox. Dr Dennis Nineham's essay in *The Myth of God Incarnate*[12] illustrates the first. We do not know enough about Jesus and the rise of Christianity for it to be possible to tie Christianity really rigorously to him in perpetuity. Both the initial uncertainties and the subsequent historical change are too great. Christianity will never forget its debt to Jesus, but it cannot honestly pretend to be forever strictly governed by him.

The other possibility, which I have myself urged, is that Christianity should be more rigorously tied than it has been in the past to what we do know of Jesus: in particular the view of God and man's relation to God implicit in his teaching. This latter I believe to be recoverable and still of the very highest religious value. But I regard as comparatively uninteresting the bulk of the historic doctrine of Christ – the incarnation, the atonement, the resurrection and ascension and so on. Those ideas, *as commonly understood*, have little to do with Jesus himself, whom I see as the supreme prophet of man's relation to God. So I envisage a Christianity that is Jewish, prophetic and existentialist, having been purged of the mythology and dogmatism superimposed upon it in the Christendom period.

Both these solutions are heretical. They agree in accepting that we do not know enough about Jesus to sustain the grandiose orthodox cycle of mythological-dogmatic beliefs about him. Thereafter they go in opposite directions.

## 4.6 *The Jewish Jesus*

In his Hebrew novel *A Guest for the Night,* S. Y. Agnon's narrator, a Polish Orthodox Jew, has money worries. He is reminded of his grandfather, who never had such troubles:

My grandfather, may he rest in peace ... never counted his money in his life, because the sages said: 'There is no blessing except in what is hidden from the eye.' So, if a poor man approached him, he would put his hand in his pocket and give. At first he would look at the money he had brought up, to see how much that poor man was worth to the Holy One, blessed be He; when he grew older he did not look, but put his hand in his pocket and gave. He used to say, 'What have you to do with the secrets of the Merciful One?'

This Orthodox Jew instinctively knows the meaning of a saying in the Sermon on the Mount which has often perplexed Christians:

When you give alms, do not let your left hand know what your right hand is doing, so that your alms may be in secret; and your Father who sees in secret will reward you (Matthew 6.3-4).

There can be no question of direct influence, for Orthodox Jews never mentioned Jesus' name, and regarded the New Testament as a forbidden book. For them the principle comes from the Talmud. A rabbi who lived at the end of the New Testament period said that 'He who gives alms in secret is greater than Moses our Teacher.' The religious meaning is that the things of God are secret and unquantifiable, and a truly religious morality is at the opposite extreme from the knowing utilitarian and technical calculations which dominate the modern secular mind. We have to go to the Jews to learn the point.

Almost all the teaching ascribed to Jesus in the synoptic gospels has been paralleled in the Talmud in this way. What Christians call the Sermon on the Mount and regard as mysterious and well-nigh impossibly exalted is to a considerable extent mysterious only because it is standard Jewish ethics rather than Christian ethics.

All of which is simply to say that Jesus was a Jew, and a figure who has at least as much in common with modern Jews as he has with modern Christians. He lived his whole life within Judaism, and there is no evidence at all that he saw himself as founder of a new religion. The idea is unthinkable. I have heard the Lord's Prayer used at Jewish-Christian gatherings, and there is no doubt that it is quite as acceptable and intelligible to Jews as to Christians.

The Jewishness of Jesus is one of those clichés which, if fully understood, calls for a considerable revision of deeply-entrenched attitudes. More recently, since the Second World War, scholars have moved on to examine the sensitive issue of the Jewishness of Paul and the relation of his theology to the Judaism of his day. It is becoming clear that a large part of Christian theology has defined itself by contrast with a monstrous caricature of Judaism.

The false antitheses are all too familiar: Jewish law demanded a merely external obedience, whereas Jesus required purity of heart; the Jewish God is remote, jealous and forbidding, whereas the Christian God is close and loving; the Jew is a slave, the Christian a son; the Jew hoped for salvation by works, the Christian receives salvation by faith; the Jew was bound by ritual and tradition, whereas Christian faith is free and spiritual – and so on. It is not surprising that centuries of this kind of propaganda should have made Jews somewhat touchy, and that they should be tempted to regard Christianity as antisemitic through and through. Modern correction of these antitheses will entail a revision of Christian theology and a change in Jewish-Christian relations. It will have to be asked whether it is right to think of Judaism and Christianity as distinct religions at all.

It is commonly thought that the main stumbling-block in the way of better Jewish-Christian relations is the Christian belief in the full coequal divinity of Jesus. For example, in 1799 the main originator of the Reform Movement in Judaism, David Friedländer (1756-1834) actually petitioned the Lutheran Church authorities in Berlin to admit him and his associates to the church, provided that they be excused from believing in Jesus' divinity and from practising distinctively Christian rites. The petition was rejected, and after the appalling history of modern antisemitism such boldness is unlikely to be soon repeated. But there are still some who say that if Christian theologians could gradually persuade the churches to be less rigid on the incarnation, and if the Jews would for their part accept the church's gentile mission, with baptism and the eucharist as full and proper gentile equivalents of circumcision and the Passover, then the ancient schism might gradually be healed.

Unfortunately it is not quite as easy as that. The original issue between Jews and Christians was not the divinity of Jesus but the messiahship of Jesus, as the New Testament makes clear. Christian theologians, or rather a few of them, may be willing to drop the divinity of Jesus as a secondary and unnecessary development of the original faith, but they cannot drop his messiahship.

Is there any chance of progress, then? There is still one card left to play. Christians do not say that the full splendour of the messianic age has already begun. The earliest faith was rather that Jesus' exaltation as Messiah began with the resurrection and is still hidden. What the early Christians were saying in their disputes with the Jews was not so much: 'The Messiah has come, for Jesus in his earthly life *was* the Messiah and you have missed the boat', but rather: 'The earthly human Jesus has shown what the messianic age will be like, and now God has exalted him as Messiah and Lord. He is the shape of our final hope.'

This narrows the disagreement. The Jew says the coming Messiah will be David-like, and the Christian says he will be Jesus-like. It is a sad irony that, at any rate before modern Zionism arose, traditional Jewish piety and hope were in many ways more Jesus-like than either Jews or Christians realized.

I have stated the issue in the now-archaic traditional terms. Many modern Jews do not expect the coming of the Messiah, and many modern Christians do not expect the second advent of Jesus, in such a literal sense as used to be accepted. But both faiths are led forward by the ideal of a perfect society of human beings under God. Eschatological hope for a perfect world must remain in some form. If it is true that Jesus' message and hope are wholly Jewish and yet are of final authority for Christians too, then he must in the end draw the two faiths together as he becomes better known.

## 4.7 *The Jesus of history and the Christ of faith*

We have taken four aspects of the critical picture of Jesus. He was a human figure, dominated by eschatological ideas and only to a limited extent accessible to us, but in so far as he *is* accessible, thoroughly Jewish. The teaching ascribed to him can be paralleled in detail in the Jewish sources.

Why then do the gospels report sharp Jewish opposition to Jesus during his own lifetime? What features of his message could have been considered heretical or blasphemous? It is not easy to say, and most scholars believe that a great deal of the conflict is the result of back-projection. At the time when the gospels were taking shape (AD 50-100) there was sharp Jewish-Christian hostility, and the early Christians supposed that Jesus must have already faced in his time charges such as they were facing in theirs.

This theory can be supported by a great many considerations. The most important point is that the back-projection has been done clumsily and is unconvincing. Thus when Jesus warns his disciples in detail about future Jewish-Christian troubles in Mark 13.9ff., the words seem incongruous and anachronistic. They have been put on Jesus' lips with the aim of encouraging a later generation, but he could not himself have thought in terms of future *history* and a split between two religions.

A classic case is the exchange between Jesus and the High Priest at his 'trial', reported in Mark 14.61f. As the commentators point out, almost everything that could be wrong with this story *is* wrong. The Sanhedrin, the supreme Jewish court, could not have met in such circumstances, could not have passed a capital sentence at one sitting, could not have considered a claim to messiahship blasphemous, and if it *had* convicted Jesus on a *religious* charge would surely itself have ordered his execution by stoning rather than remit the case to the Roman authorities. (The gospels say it lacked the right; but this is doubtful.) Perhaps the most telling and simple point is this: the High Priest could not possibly *himself* have used the odd phrase 'the Son of the Blessed' in any *special technical Christian sense* such as Jews might have found *religiously* offensive. No such sense yet existed, or (if that is thought question-begging) it could not have existed so far as the Jewish High Priest was concerned. 'Son of God' was a stock Jewish phrase (e.g., Matthew 5.9).

From these and many other instances we must conclude that later Jewish-Christian hostilities have been projected back into the gospel story. There was a marked tendency to shift the blame for Jesus' death from the Romans to the Jews. In the gospel-writing period the church was making great theological claims on Jesus' behalf, and this was giving rise to controversy with those Jews who refused to accept the claims. Christians were being driven out of the synagogues. Writing the gospels, the early Christians naturally suggested that Jesus, 30 to 60 years earlier, had already been making similar claims, had met opposition to them, had been thrown out of the synagogue and had suffered rejection and condemnation by his own people.

Fortunately, the job of back-projection was not done completely consistently. We can discount it because of the differences between the gospels and the internal inconsistencies within them. For example, we note the different treatments of Pilate in the different gospels, and the ambiguities of the gospel treatment of the Pharisees. We find Pharisees approving Jesus' teaching, entertaining him, and warning him of danger – and all this alongside the most virulent blanket condemnation of Pharisaism. It does not add up, and the best theory to account for it is the theory of back-projection.

But discounting back-projection in this way only worsens the problem faced by Christian theologians. How can we explain, and still more how can we *justify*, the transition from the Jesus of history to the Christ of faith?

The distinction between the Jesus of history and the Christ of faith began to be clearly made in the second half of the nineteenth century. The Jesus of history, or historical Jesus, is simply the man who lived as he is pictured by the critical historian – Galilean Jew, itinerant radical holy man, teacher, healer and prophet of the Kingdom of God. The Christ of faith is the one postulated by Christian faith and described in the creeds – an eternal heavenly, and perhaps divine, being who descended to earth, took flesh in Mary's womb, lived among men, suffered and died for our salvation, rose from the dead, ascended into heaven, sits at the right hand of God, and now reigns over the entire universe.

Traditionally it has of course been believed that the two were and are identical, which is why many people find the distinction puzzling. But the more we look at the synoptic gospels the more we seem obliged to make the distinction. These gospels do not present Jesus as the earthly incarnation of a pre-existent being. The annunciation-stories in Matthew and Luke seem to say that Jesus' birth, like the births of Isaac or Samuel in the Old Testament, is the divinely-ordained birth of a great charismatic (that is, specially graced or gifted) *human* figure. The same gospels do not seem to present Jesus as saying that the only way to approach God is through himself, but rather that man must turn to God directly and without a mediator. And again, there is rather *little* evidence in the gospels of the developed Christian idea of Jesus' death as the necessary atonement for all human sin (Mark 10.45 is the main exception), and there is *no* evidence that Jesus taught or believed in his own divinity.

It is hard to avoid the conclusion that the religion Jesus himself believed and taught was very different from the later Christian religion ostensibly based on Jesus. The contrast between the two religions derives mainly from the fact that Jesus did not believe in original sin. He followed the prophets in holding that the individual can and must turn directly to God in repentance and faith, and can gain God's forgiveness directly. There is no insuperable barrier between man and God. God is close to man and offers forgiveness freely. Of course Jesus' God is holy and exalted and strange, and the relation to God is as demanding as could be. There is nothing easy about Jesus' religion. But neither is it impossible.

According to Christianity, though, man is trapped and bound in original sin and cannot properly perform the initial act of turning to God. Only if we cleave to the Mediator, a divine-human being who bridges the gulf between God and man, can we gain the promise of God's forgiveness and the prospect of eternal salvation in the world to come. Jesus is identified with this Mediator.

So the confusing irony is this, that Jesus, the Jewish teacher of an *immediate* relation between man and God, became incorporated into a religion which says the opposite of what he taught. Christianity said that Christ is the only one who can bridge the mighty gulf between God and man, and God's forgiveness can only be obtained *via* him. Where Jesus taught his disciples to pray directly to Our Father, the church of Jesus prays to Almighty and Everlasting God through Jesus Christ our Lord.

It is a puzzle, and it is particularly difficult for incarnational-ists. Following the modern version of the doctrine of the incarnation, we might say that God has made his own the humanity of a humble first-century Jew, a man of his time whose outlook is inevitably in some ways dated, and so on. But it is not easy to think of any good reason why the man in whom God is incarnate should have been so misguided as to teach a religion which on the Christian view is just plain wrong. For as the Lord's Prayer indicates, Jesus' religion held that though it is very costly to do so, we must above all else turn directly to God and receive God's forgiveness directly. Whereas the Christian religion says, 'That will not work. Man cannot turn to God directly, but must cleave to the Mediator. Only Jesus was free from original sin, so only Jesus can relate himself to God immediately. *Jesus' religion applies only to himself.* Everyone else must go *via* Jesus, because God only bestows forgiveness *via* Jesus.'

That is really confusing: a mediating religion focussed around a man whose own religion was immediate.

## 4.8 *Demythologizing*

In 1941 Rudolf Bultmann published an essay called 'New Testament and Mythology' which gave rise to a long and heated controversy.

Bultmann pointed out that the New Testament writers take for granted a mythological outlook which is quite unreal to moderns who accept the scientific view of the world. The difference between them and us affects such basic categories as space, time, causality and human personality. So far as space is concerned, they thought in terms of a three-decker universe with Heaven above the Earth and Hell below it. Christ can 'descend' or 'ascend' from one zone to another. As for time, they supposed that the present historical order would very soon be spectacularly demolished by God and a new order would be set up in its place. With respect to causality, they assumed that events in the physical world can be and often are brought about by the action of invisible supernatural forces. As for human personality, many New Testament writers seem able to think of Jesus as having been *both* a man who grew, learned, was tempted and suffered *and* a pre-existent heavenly being who had come into the world.

Because of our post-Darwinian biological understanding of how human personality develops we find this incredible, but in earlier times it made more sense because *every* human being's soul or spirit was in a way thought of as coming from God or belonging to the heavenly world.

So Bultmann said that modern theology must strip off the obsolete mythology in which the New Testament gospel is packaged. You might object that the mythology *is* the gospel: strip it off and nothing is left. Bultmann did not agree. As a Lutheran, he located the gospel mainly in the preaching or *kerygma* (Greek for 'proclamation') of the primitive church, and in particular in St Paul's teaching. St Paul's doctrine is, according to Bultmann, mainly about man – man in sin, man under grace; man bound and free, man judged and saved. When the core of the gospel has been freed of its mythological wrappings what we find is a message about human existence which can be rephrased in the language of existentialist philosophy.

Why existentialist philosophy? As a German Lutheran, Bultmann stands in the tradition of Kant and Kierkegaard. Objective knowledge of the natural world is the business of natural science, which has a monopoly; and it has nothing to say about religion and morality. Religion and morality belong within the sphere of man's subjectivity, as he considers what to do with his freedom, what to make of himself and how to live. So God's action upon the world takes place at one point only, the point where there is a change in the individual human person's self-understanding and way of living.

Luther in the sixteenth century and Wesley in the eighteenth had already gone a long way towards 'internalizing' Christianity – translating it into, or cashing it in terms of, the inner life of the individual and his religious experience. Bultmann the ultra-Protestant goes further still, discarding the whole cosmological, public and objective dimension of religion. For us in the age of science it has become a requirement of rationality that the world be seen as one seamless, continuous natural process. Natural explanation is complete and requires no theological overlay. Christianity is no longer an explanation of the world: it is a way to live. For example, the statement that 'God made the world' means, on Bultmann's account, 'I live best when I regard my whole life and all that happens to me as God's gift.'

So existentialist philosophy was Bultmann's natural ally. It showed the only way in which moral and religious values can be conserved in a world dominated by secular science. It provided a vocabulary in terms of which Bultmann could restate the gospel in 'demythologized' terms. Secular existentialists make a distinction between a bad attitude to life in which we are in bondage to the world, drift with the crowd and are afraid to be truly free, and a good attitude to life in which we break out of bondage to the past, the world and the mob and begin to live truly free, open and autonomous lives. This is close to St Paul's contrast between man in sin and man under grace. Here is a way in which we can state Christianity in a form that is intelligible today and is free from obsolete language and assumptions. Bultmann's own short statement of the gospel as it might be preached to industrial workers is given in *The Honest to God Debate*, edited by John A. T. Robinson and David L. Edwards. [13]

It follows from all this that Bultmann and his school have regarded the incarnation as a mythological idea for a couple of generations. The present controversies in Britain have a long prehistory. Bultmann was violently attacked from many points of view: for having too crude an idea of myth, for taking the scientific outlook too literally, for not demythologizing God out altogether and becoming a secular existentialist, and so on. The literature of the controversy is enormous, but it need not further concern us for the present. [14]

One point, however, is vitally important. Bultmann was not going back behind the Christ of faith to the Jesus of history. He thought that that programme had been attempted by nineteenth-century liberals and had proved a failure. The real

Jesus had been a Jewish and pre-Christian figure, very strange and remote and even less intelligible to us than the theology of St Paul. What Bultmann did was demythologize Paul's relatively developed theology and find underneath it something that could be re-expressed in the language of existentialist philosophy.

There are here two quite different ideas of how Christianity became mythicized. In the English-speaking countries we tend to see Jesus the man as having been posthumously mythicized into the Christ of the creeds. But for Bultmann it is the conversion-experience (life in sin, the transition, and the new life) which St Paul describes in mythicized terms. This conversion experience – the gospel proclaimed and the change it brings about in the believer – came into being after Easter and is for Bultmann the nucleus of Christianity. Like other theologians of his generation he was not particularly interested in the Jewish historical Jesus. The New Testament is a post-Jesus book which everywhere presupposes the entirely new situation created by the birth of the Easter faith. Thus the historical Jesus is no more than a shadow in the background of Christianity.

For some people Christianity needs to be demythologized because it is deeply inconsistent with Jesus, but that does not worry Bultmann. He demythologizes Christianity in order to make it intelligible to modern man. In assessing modern controversy about the doctrine of the incarnation we must carefully distinguish two assertions: (*a*) that it is an intrinsically mythological and unacceptable idea; and (*b*) that it is an idea incompatible with Jesus himself, being part of a later superstructure erected over him.


### 4.9 *Religious truth and cultural change*

Plato made a distinction between two different worlds to which we have access, a distinction which has haunted Western thought ever since.

All around us is the natural world, the world of sense, the world that appears to us. It is unstable and in constant change and our knowledge of it has a correspondingly shifting, imperfect and inconclusive character. But in addition there is the world of pure thought, eternal and unchangeable, populated by purely intelligible realities. Of this higher world we can have genuine, certain knowledge.

Plato's theory suggested that theology is a body of certain, timelessly true knowledge of eternal verities.

A more recent version of a similar distinction draws the line between truths of reason and truths of fact. Truths of reason, such as the principles of logic and mathematics, are knowable *a priori* (independently of experience). They are shown by demonstration, by their own self-evidence or by definition. Mathematical statements, for example, are either necessarily true or necessarily false. They are neither affected by experience nor eroded by the passage of time. If true, they are true always and everywhere for all intellects. Since some people hold that basic moral principles have a similar absolute and unconditional validity, they too have been thought to be true *a priori*.

Truths of fact, by contrast, are based on experience and concern the worlds of nature and history. Here we are concerned only with probabilities, not absolute certainties, and reason is typically inductive rather than deductive. In our empirical knowledge there is a very important interplay between the facts and the various theories we devise in order to show up, organize and explain the facts. Different theories draw attention to different facts and give them different significances. So knowledge grows not only by accumulating more facts but also by continuously generating and trying out new theories. In natural science we call this 'the scientific method', and in the humanities 'the critical method'. Our knowledge is a provisional, continually-changing human construction.

Which of these two kinds of knowledge does religious belief most resemble? Conservatives today like to put it in the first category, but liberal or critical theologians see more and more reasons for putting it in the second.

The traditionalists hold that religious truth is certain and immutable because it is about God and comes from God, who has revealed it and is himself immutable. Thus Eastern Orthodox Christians speak of Holy Orthodox Tradition as perfect and immutable, Catholics of the church as *semper eadem*, 'always the same', and Protestants of scripture as God's written Word to men. People who think in this way will probably also claim that moral principles are 'absolute', that is, eternally and immutably true. The doctrine of the incarnation of God in Christ fits rather well into this general outlook, because it gives the world of eternal truths a bridgehead in the world of transient fact. At this point the eternal and unchangeable established itself in history.

But is it really being claimed that the primary data of Christianity – Jesus' life, the words of the New Testament, the doctrines of the creed – have the same sort of status as the axioms of a formal system like Euclid's geometry? Some people have come near to saying so, especially in the seventeenth century, a very rationalist period. Jesus was said to be absolute in every human perfection – physical beauty, wisdom, goodness and skill in all the arts and sciences. If his life has that sort of absoluteness, it would seem that everyone who seeks to imitate him should become a celibate male wandering preacher and exorcist, which is hard on housewives. In the same period the primary data of Christianity *were* treated as axioms from which Christian doctrine was deduced geometrically. So there is no innovation in all church history, only the deduction of fresh consequences from the initial revealed axioms. If you had asked St Paul whether he believed in the Bodily Assumption of Mary into heaven he would after a few moments thought have said that of course that doctrine was strictly implied by things he already believed.

Such ways of thinking were shattering by the rise of the historical consciousness. To a historian the Christian tradition is only one of several, and every particular human product, whether it be a life lived, beliefs held, texts written, artefacts made or rites performed, has a *provenance:* that is, it belongs to and is part of one particular and unique historical and cultural context. Everything human has a period flavour, all periods are different, and each has to be understood in its own terms. Nothing passes from one period to another without any change at all. You almost have to say that an old book like the New Testament is a different book in each period, because what people see in it and make of it changes so much in successive ages.

It follows that Jesus' life and message have to be understood historically, i.e. in the context of their own time. If he had lived in a different place and time he would not have been the same person and he could neither have lived just the same life nor taught just the same message. When we noticed an eighteenth-century German writer commenting that 'Angels belonged to the theological machinery of the Jews', we saw the influence of the historical consciousness. And not only angels, but the entire conceptual apparatus of the New Testament is similarly peculiar to its own time and could not be just the same, nor have just the same meaning, at any other time.

So Christian belief cannot be a coherent system of timeless truths revealed at one moment in past history, because there cannot be any such thing. Religious truth cannot be permanently packaged: it has to be reminted, rediscovered in every succeeding age, because man is immersed in history like a fish in water.

Several of the authors of *The Myth of God Incarnate*, particularly Dr Dennis Nineham, Mr J. L. Houlden and to a lesser extent Professor Maurice Wiles, emphasize these points very strongly. The German writer who made them with most force was Ernst Troeltsch (1865-1923). Conservatives react with considerable hostility, saying that this position implies a degree of historical relativism so extreme as to destroy rationality altogether and made each age the prisoner of its own assumptions.

This reply is unfair. The historical point of view does not make the past inaccessible: it only says that we have to use historical imagination to understand it. Nor does it deny orginality and greatness: it says only that creative originality is always exercised in relation to a particular cultural context. We can obviously understand Shakespeare – but we must understand his plays in the context of their time; and we can recognize his originality and greatness – against their background. That Shakespeare does not transcend history *altogether* soon becomes obvious when we recognize things in the plays (such as his supernatural apparatus, or his attitude to the Jews), which we very definitely do not share. To have the historical consciousness is liberating. It is the literalist who falls into gross mistakes.

Still, Troeltsch and those moderns who are influenced by him are right to say that the historical consciousness does destroy fundamentalist kinds of religion.

# 5

# Does the New Testament Teach the Divinity of Christ?

## 5.1 *Monotheism assumed*

At the time when the New Testament was written the popular colloquial language of much of the Mediterranean world was a dialect form of Greek. The New Testament is written in this dialect, with a strong Jewish accent containing echoes of the Hebrew Bible and in some places of Jesus' own language, Palestinian Aramaic. The social setting of the New Testament is the fringe of diaspora Judaism, and early Christianity was an unorthodox Jewish sect.

The writings in the New Testament are very miscellaneous. From the historian's point of view it seems a mere contingent fact that some early Christian writings survived and not others, some were believed to be directly or indirectly 'apostolic' and not others, and some came to be reckoned canonical and not others.

The canonical writings were not consciously written as scripture. They are occasional, being addressed to contemporary groups and individuals with contemporary issues in mind rather than to the world in general or to posterity. They do not profess to be by God, and nobody claims to be God's mouthpiece by uttering the old formula, 'Thus says the Lord. . . .'

All the writings take for granted a background in Jewish faith, and the scriptures appealed to are the Jewish scriptures, either the Hebrew Bible or the Greek translation of it which includes the Apocrypha and is called the *Septuagint*.

All this means that the God of the New Testament is the God of Israel, and where God is spoken of as 'God the Father' or 'the Father' it is again simply the God of Israel who is being spoken of.

It can sometimes happen on earth that monarchy is shared. At times there were two and even three emperors within the one Roman Empire, each responsible for a different region. Again, it once happened in England that two persons, William and Mary, were jointly sovereign. But Jewish faith in God rules out any arrangement of this kind. It was held that God, the God of Israel, is absolutely sole and his power cannot be divided or coequally shared. The New Testament writers never question this principle and nowhere think of themselves as possibly infringing it. They never distinguish coequal persons within the one God: the idea was unthinkable. It was also unthinkable to say that Jesus was identical with the one God. So it is very difficult to see how they could even have entertained the ideas of the divinity of Christ and the Trinity. The drastic modification of the doctrine of God and the formulation of new concepts (divine person, divine nature etc.) which would eventually be undertaken had not even begun.

So when a New Testament writer speaks of 'God the Father and the Lord Jesus Christ', how is he to be understood? He does *not* mean something like William and Mary, jointly sovereign. Nor does he mean something like the Eastern Roman Emperor and the Western Roman Emperor, co-rulers of an empire divided for administrative and defence purposes. What he means is something much more like 'The King, and the King's Ambassador', God and the one who reveals, speaks for and represents God.

To prove the point we have to read some New Testament writings with that model in mind, and we find in general that it fits. In the Old Testament religion there was a great variety of different kinds of men of God: prophets who spoke for God, priests who regulated society's relation to God, wise men who were spiritual masters and ethical teachers, and kings who ruled Israel under God. If we could imagine one comprehensive figure who united all these functions and was plenipotentiary in all God's dealings with men, that would be the figure that the New Testament writers take Christ to be. Such a figure is not himself God except in the very restricted sense that an ambassador is royal and may in certain formal contexts be treated *as if* he were the King.

An ambassador is in a sense royal, but is not himself the King. By paying certain royal honours to the ambassador you do not question or detract from the sole monarchy of the King he represents: on the contrary, you affirm it. To honour the ambassador is to honour not the ambassador himself but the King he stands for.

This model suggests how it was possible for the early Christians to use extremely exalted language about Christ without feeling that they might possibly be infringing monotheism. If we use the model as a guiding thread in the discussion that follows then the extremely complex New Testament language about Christ may begin to make sense; but of course we must be critical and not dogmatic, which means that we do not impose the model on the evidence, but use it as a hypothesis and look out for any points at which it breaks down. To be truly scientific about religious thought we must always look for the difficulties.

One point of detail is significant. Unlike English, Greek makes a distinction between 'God' without an article in front of it, and 'the God', with an article. Without an article, the word 'God' is being used predicatively, and has rather the same meaning as the English adjective 'divine'. Thus in John 1.1, 'the Word was God' means roughly, 'the Word was divine'. With the article, 'the God' means God the Father, the God of Israel, Yahweh, God the unique individual as known by his proper name. So in the same verse, 'the Word was with (*the*) God' means 'the Word was with God the Father'. The distinction between these two ways of using the word

'God' is important, but unfortunately the English language does not mark it clearly. As a result, our English translations of John 1.1 read, very confusingly: 'The Word was with God, and the Word was God.' It would be less misleading to translate: 'the Word was with the Father, and the Word was divine.'

However, even this will not quite do as a translation because it could suggest that there is a class of divine beings, of whom the Father is one and the Word another; whereas for all Jews, including the early Christians, there is only one God. To avoid this difficulty the line ought to be retranslated, 'The Word was with God the Father and the Word was the Father's own Word', to stress that the Word is not an *independent* divine being but is the only God's own self-expression.

If all this is correct, then even John's language about Jesus still falls within the scope of the King-ambassador model, though the model is here coming under some strain. And John's doctrine raises the general problem of intermediary beings.

## 5.2  *Intermediary beings*

For a very long time Christians have told a certain story about the religious life of late ancient Judaism between the fifth century BC and the rise of Christianity. It runs like this:

After the Jews returned from exile the voice of prophecy died away and religion was increasingly dominated by the Book, the Torah. God seemed more and more remote. People sought to please God by obeying the Law. If they thought they were succeeding they became self-righteous and arrogant, but if they thought they were failing they fell a prey to tormenting anxiety. So they oscillated between pride and despair, because they lacked personal communion with God and immediate experience of God's grace. And that (it was implied) is the condition of Judaism as a religion to this day. Because God was remote various intermediary beings were postulated in order to link God to the world – angels, the Torah itself imagined as a heavenly being, the Wisdom of God, the Presence or Glory (Shekinah) of God, and so on. In addition, there were various conceptions of the perfect Man – the Heavenly Adam, the Son of Man and so on. All these conceptions were eventually to find their proper fulfilment in the Christian doctrine of Christ, for he is the perfect Man, the true heavenly intermediary and the one in whom man's ideal relation to God is at last realized. Thus Christianity solves the religious problem of Judaism, and fulfils and supersedes it.

This story is a myth, because it is a *validating* story told by Christians to show that their own faith surpasses Judaism. It is often told with Saul, the Pharisee from Tarsus who became St Paul the Christian, as its hero.

Some elements in it are true. There were these intermediary beings, and they did influence early ideas about Christ. One of the most important is Wisdom:

The Lord created me at the beginning of his work,
   the first of his acts of old.
Ages ago I was set up,
   at the first, before the beginning of the earth . . .
When he established the heavens I was there . . .
I was beside him like a master workman;
and I was daily his delight . . .
(from Proverbs 8.22–31: *c*.250 BC)

Other passages about Wisdom can be found in Job 28, and Ecclesiasticus 1.1-10 and 24. And it seems clear that St Paul's remarkable language about Christ as a pre-existent heavenly figure who had assisted at the creation of the world is influenced by these ideas. In the discussion in I Corinthians 1, he calls Christ the Wisdom of God. On closer examination we find connections running all over the place. In Jewish writings the various figures of the Wisdom of God, the Word of God, the Torah and so on seem all to be personified and to flow into each other. The words ascribed to Jesus by Matthew

(11.28ff.), 'Come unto me, all who labour and are heavy-laden, and I will give you rest' have seemed to many believers to be very personal and direct, but they turn out to be model-led on a speech by Wisdom in Ecclesiasticus (51.24-7).

What are we to make of all this? The issues are very techni-cal, but some points seem clear.

In Jewish religion God was not remote. It is a very common and very bad mistake in religious thought to equate transcen-dence with inaccessibility and remoteness. Quite the opposite is the truth. Wisdom was certainly not a friendlier, nearer substitute for God as an object of devotion. Thought about Wisdom is speculative, not religious and devotional. Wisdom was something like a prescientific idea of cosmic order, resembling the Tao in China and the Logos in Greece.

It is questionable whether the Jews really thought of the intermediaries as distinct individual beings at all. The shades of meaning are fine: was the intermediary thought of as a manifestation of God, as an emanation of God, as a being begotten by God or as a being created by God? No clear answer can be given, and many think the question badly put. The intermediaries were, they say, simply poetic and peri-phrastic (roundabout) ways of speaking about God's man-ifold action in the world. Taking the intermediaries too liter-ally only leads back to the myth from which we began this section, a myth which is now increasingly thought to be a propagandist misrepresentation of Jewish religion.

What follows for Christian theology, and the question of Jesus' divinity? It seems that we cannot realistically claim that the Second Person of the Trinity, God's coequal, coeternal Son, was already latent in Jewish religious thought. In any case, whatever the ancient Jews believed about the inter-mediaries, we do not have any reason to believe in them. All we can say is that Paul, John and others borrowed certain figures of speech in order to express their sense of the cosmic significance of the risen Jesus. But in our time we do not have available to us any ideas of a quasi-divine principle of cosmic order to borrow from. We cannot link Jesus to a cosmic principle so easily as they did.


## 5.3 *The Messiah and the Son of God*

The two most important New Testament titles of Jesus are Messiah (Greek, 'Christ') and Son of God. Both titles are very complex, raise many questions, and have deep roots in ancient Israelite faith.

Messiah, or more exactly *mashiach* in Hebrew, means 'anointed one'. It describes a person commissioned by God to perform a special task. In the Hebrew Bible prophets, priests and even a pagan king like Cyrus can be described as God's Anointed, but the typical use of the title is for the King of Israel.

The Jews believed that God had promised that David's dynasty would last for ever (II Samuel 7.8-16). After the monarchy was overthrown the hope naturally arose that one day God would keep the old promise and raise up a Son of David to re-establish the throne and restore the nation's former glory. So the Messiah was classically a purely human figure, the legitimate national king of the Jews. He was an eschatological deliverer: at the end of time and in the darkest hour he would return, bringing the final fulfilment of all Israel's national and religious hopes.

The Messiah's task was therefore basically this-worldly and even 'political'. In modern times many ultra-orthodox Jews opposed Zionism on the ground that it is a presumptuous attempt to do the Messiah's job before the Messiah has come: that is to say, in traditional Judaism the Messiah's task was precisely to realize the Zionist dream.

In Jesus' time a great range of other ideas, some of them barely compatible with each other, had also gathered around the figure of the Messiah. The gospels suggest that messianic rumours and hopes gathered around Jesus, that he himself was extremely wary of the title of Messiah, and that he

thought of the New Age as coming into being by the supernatural action of God rather than by the political action of any
merely human figure. So he preferred to describe the
eschatological deliverer-figure as 'the Son of Man', a
heavenly figure who would descend to earth. His own relation to the Son of Man is a puzzle: was he *already* the Son of
Man, would he return as the Son of Man, or was the Son of
Man a character distinct from himself? It is uncertain, but the
main point is that Jesus saw the coming great Event not so
much as the victory of an earthly Messiah-figure, but rather
as the descent from God of a glorious Son of Man figure.
There is also a strong tradition that the Deliverer would
achieve his task by passing through a time of terrible suffering and affliction.

If Jesus had been so cautious about the title of Messiah,
why was the early Christian community so unanimous about
it? The answer may be that in a Christian context Jesus is
already crucified. It was no longer possible to make the mistake of thinking that his earthly mission was to lead a national
liberation-struggle. He was enthroned in heaven as a Messiah
who had suffered and would return in glory ('on the clouds of
heaven') to judge the quick and the dead – in short, he was a
figure very like Jesus' own 'Son of Man'. The crucifixion had
purged the concept of messiahship and made its use in connection with Jesus acceptable.

The title 'Son of God' is still more difficult and complex. In
Israelite tradition it stood for an individual or group which
obeyed God, was close to God, and was under God's protection. Angels might be called sons of God, the nation as a
whole was God's son, and a devout believer who was a man
of God might be called God's son. But typically the title
belonged to the King of Israel (II Samuel 7.14), who is called
God's Son in the Psalms (e.g. Psalm 2).

Most Christian readers of the New Testament, when they
meet the phrase Son of God in connection with Jesus, naturally understand it to have the special technical sense that

became attached to it after the Council of Nicea. That is certainly wrong. In reaction, we might suppose that throughout the New Testament the phrase bears no more than its traditonal Jewish sense of a just and devout man close to God (as in Mark 15.39). That is also wrong, for quite clearly the New Testament writers do think that Jesus is *the* Son of God in a special sense. Bultmann and others have thought that the special New Testament sense in which Jesus is the Son of God was borrowed from paganism, where it was certainly widely used. But most scholars think this theory wrong too.

So, in conclusion, the New Testament writers *do* use the phrase 'Son of God' in a sense stronger than the traditional Jewish meaning, but *not* in the sense either of paganism or of developed Christian orthodoxy. What they mean can only be discovered by careful, unprejudiced reading of particular authors. In this matter of the title 'Son of God' it is very important not to assume in advance that we know what it means.

## 5.4 *Jesus*

Did Jesus teach his own divinity, either explicitly or implicitly? John's gospel must be set aside, because although it does contain some primitive theology it has hardly a trace of Jesus' own ways of speaking. In the synoptic gospels we have to discount what are clearly post-crucifixion ideas superimposed upon the tradition, and we have to compare the texts closely in search of the earliest forms of the various sayings. When we have done that, it is obvious that Jesus was a purely human figure: a strange character of great rhetorical brilliance, emotional vehemence and charismatic gifts, but nevertheless entirely human. It is noticeable that there is no suggestion of his pre-existence. Sayings like the following are striking:

Why do you call me good? No one is good but God alone.

(Mark 10.18)

> Who made me a judge or divider over you?
>
> (Luke 12.14)

It may even be that such sayings were included in the gospels by way of protest against a growing tendency to deify Jesus.

The main passage quoted by conservative believers is Matthew 11. 25-7 (= Luke 10.21f.). Scholars disagree about whether this passage could possibly go back to primitive and purely Palestinian circles. But whatever the answer to that question, the words seem unlikely to come from Jesus himself. They are very different in style and content from the main body of his teaching. They do *not* claim divinity, but they do embody the idea of his Sonship current in early Christian times and so seem to be of early Christian origin.

## 5.5 *The first generation*

The outlook of the first generation of Christians (AD 30-50) is tantalizingly difficult to recover. One can get a sense of it by working backwards from St Paul's early letters, by studying the development of the gospel tradition and in similar ways; but the main source is of course the Acts of the Apostles, a book whose historical value is controversial. The other sources suggest that the earliest faith was dominated by the expectation that the Kingdom of God was coming almost immediately, but Acts disposes of this idea almost at once (1. 6-8) and sets out instead to tell a story of orderly expansion under the direction of the Spirit.

However, the author of Acts (let us call him Luke), does not lack historical awareness. Conservative scholars in today's controversies often stigmatize ideas of doctrinal development and evolution as Victorian, and claim that the idea of Jesus' divinity was implicit from the very first. It didn't develop gradually, but was there from the beginning. But Luke seems to have the idea of doctrinal development. He is rather careful to show the evolution from the primitive Jewish church at Jerusalem towards the infant Gentile church, breaking away from Judaism. The members of the new community are at first called the disciples (1.15, Western text), the brethren (1.16), those that believed (2.44) and the saved (2.47). The term 'church' first appears at 5.11, and 'Christians' in Antioch at 11.26. Jewish observances and the maintenance of continuity with Judaism are stressed in early chapters but fade later. Peter gives place to Paul.

If we go through the text underlining all the titles and brief doctrinal statements linked with Jesus we get a somewhat similar picture. Jesus is first called Lord after the Ascension (1.21), and Christ after Pentecost (2.36). In Peter's primitive Jerusalem church Jesus is called Jesus Christ of Nazareth (3.6), the Holy and Righteous One (3.14), prophet (3.22f.), Leader and Saviour (5.31): but the most typical primitive title Luke quotes is God's holy Servant (3.13, 26; 4.27, 30), the Greek word *pais* being that used by the Septuagint in translating the Servant-poems of Isaiah. Jesus is first called 'Son of God' in Syria by Paul (9.20; 8.37 is not original). As the story moves out to the Gentile world, with Paul as the central character, the titles Servant, Prophet, Holy and Righteous One and Leader vanish.

It certainly looks as if Luke has a historical sense and attributes a distinctive view of Jesus to the earliest Jewish church. Throughout the book, indeed, there is no hint of the doctrine of the incarnation. Jesus is not a pre-existent being descended to earth but a man appointed by God and anointed by the Spirit for a unique vocation and destiny. The only allusions to the belief that a man might be a god are highly pejorative (12.22; 14.11).

What we can glean elsewhere of the beliefs of the first generation broadly fits with this picture. Jesus was a man born by the providence of God, a prophet and servant of God destined to be the Messiah of Israel, who had been rejected and crucified. But God had raised him to a heavenly throne where he now reigned as Lord, Christ and Son of God, and would very shortly appear in glory.

### 5.6 *Matthew, Mark and Luke*

The synoptic gospel-writers present Jesus as a human figure, modelled on such great Old Testament heroes as Moses and Elijah. Though greater than they, he is a being of the same kind, namely a man raised up and commissioned by God to perform a special task. The Messiah and the Son of God are in these gospels generally human, earthly figures. The Son of Man is, sometimes at least, a heavenly figure, but not divine. The pre-existence of Jesus seems not to be taught, though he *is* thought of as predestined to his vocation.

Of the three, the one that comes nearest to teaching Jesus' divinity is St Mark, for whom the phrase 'Son of God' does seem sometimes to have an almost divine resonance. However historically inaccurate he is in so thinking, Mark seems to suppose that there was something about Jesus' Sonship, authority and powers which could give rise to charges of blasphemy on the part of his critics. In 2.7 Jesus' power to dispense forgiveness attracts such a charge; but Jesus does not accept the implication that he is claiming divinity, merely saying that God has given the Son of Man – presumably Jesus refers to himself – authority to dispense God's forgiveness. At 12.6, in the parable, the son is given a different status from the servants who preceded him, which may possibly indicate that Mark believed in Jesus' divinity. In 14.61-4, which we have discussed already, the High Priest's question and his response to Jesus' answer may indicate that Mark thought the phrase 'the Christ, the Son of the Blessed' carried implications of divinity, though the jeering command 'Prophesy!' in verse 65 suggest that Jesus is being arraigned merely as a false prophet.

I must repeat what has been said already, that these examples will not stand up historically. There is no good reason to think that Jesus himself claimed to possess divine powers in his own right, or to be the Son of God in some sense that implied his own divinity. We are concerned only with what *Mark* thought, rightly or wrongly. And it is possible that Mark can be described as believing in the divinity of Christ, though he also includes in his gospel a good deal that tells the other way.

Matthew and Luke do not go any further than Mark, and even (especially in Luke's case) pull back a little. Their birth-stories actually tell against the idea of incarnation, for what they describe is a human birth brought about by God's Spirit and modelled on similar stories in the Old Testament. Jesus is given a human genealogy which sets him in the great line of men of God, 'the holy seed'. It is not a case of an unprecedented descent of God to take human flesh, but rather a case of God's Spirit again acting to ensure the conception of the last of the line. The virginity of Mary is not stressed in order to make the point that Jesus is a hybrid being who has God for a father and a human woman for his mother. Indeed, he is elsewhere presented as a carpenter's son who is descended from David through his human father. Probably the original purpose of the birth-narratives was to say simply that it was fitting that the Holy One should be born of a pure maiden of the House of Israel.

A few other lines from Matthew deserve brief mention. The name Emmanuel (1.23) does not imply Jesus' divinity for it did not imply it in the situation of Isaiah's original prophecy, and theophoric (God-bearing) names were common among the Jews. The story of Jesus' baptism is messianic: Sonship is a task to which Jesus has just been appointed rather than a status which he has enjoyed from all eternity. The temptation stories that follow test his fitness for that task. In 9.8 Matthew develops Mark's view of the incident: the power of forgiveness is not at all a sign of Jesus' divine status, for it is being poured out upon men in general. The exalted hymn in 11.25-7 is, as we have already noted, probably not from Jesus himself, but it shows that for Matthew Jesus was *the* Son in the full sense, given plenary authority by God, and the true and final way to God. But Jesus' divinity is not strictly implied by this.

In 16.13-20, the confession at Caesarea Philippi, Matthew goes beyond Mark, for Jesus here endorses Peter's confession. But it is clear from the context that the phrase 'the Son of the living God' just means Messiah, and no more. The puzzling little exchange in 22.41-5, reported by all three evangelists, seems to say that the Messiah is David's Lord and not David's son. It is puzzling because many early Christians were keen to prove Jesus David's son, but in any case it need mean no more than that Jesus is to be a heavenly Lord-Messiah rather than an earthly king. At 24.36 we note that the phrase 'nor the Son', taken from Mark, is missing in some manuscripts of Matthew. As it stands the verse reflects early Christian anxiety about just when the End would come. If Matthew or Mark or both originally included the phrase 'nor the Son', then it tells *against* their belief in Jesus' divinity, for it is saying 'there are some things God doesn't tell even Jesus'.

Finally, Matthew's baptismal formula (28.19) has been mentioned already. It is of late origin, and in any case ought not to be read anachronistically as evidence that Matthew believed in a coequal Trinity.

Luke adds little to the points we have already noted in Matthew and Mark. In 3.38 he calls Adam the son of God. In 7.16 the cry that 'God has visited his people!' is a traditional metaphor, which follows naturally from the previous exclamation, 'A great prophet has arisen among us!' The voice at the Transfiguration in 9.35, by putting 'my Chosen' in apposition to 'my Son', suggests that Jesus' sonship is a matter of divine appointment rather than eternal nature.

So the generalization that the synoptic gospels do not teach the divinity of Christ is on the whole sound. Mark comes nearest, but he is not unambiguous. The Son of God is to

God as an ambassador is to the King he represents. Jesus is
the one appointed by God to bring in and reign over the age
of salvation; but the gospels come nowhere near to saying
that he is Very God of Very God.


## 5.7 *Paul*

Half the books in the New Testament are traditionally credited to St Paul, which is at least a testimony to the great
prestige of his name. How many are truly his is disputed. The
nucleus that few question consists of the first four: Romans,
I and II Corinthians and Galatians. For our present purposes
we may also include the next five in the canon, Ephesians to
II Thessalonians, together with the little note to Philemon.

For Paul, Jesus is obviously Lord, Christ (almost as a sur-
name rather than as an office) and Son of God in the strong
sense: *the* Son, God's heavenly companion, enthroned at
God's right hand. The historical Jesus and the vocabulary
associated with him seem to have receded into the background, and all the emphasis is on the Son Jesus Christ as
exalted cosmic Lord.

But we should not too quickly assume that Paul therefore
believes in the divinity of Christ. For in his writings *God the
Father* and *the Son, the Lord Jesus Christ* are always two distinct
beings, very closely associated but never simply identified.
The relation between them is something like that between
King and ambassador, employer and omnicompetent secretary, or Sultan and Grand Vizier. Christ is God's right hand
man: all God does, he does through Christ, and all approach
to God is through Christ. All traffic, both ways, between God
and the world is routed through Christ.

It follows that faith-union with Christ is the only way to
salvation. Paul appears to believe that the traditional Jewish
religion (based on God's election, the covenant between God
and Israel, the gift of the Law and the sufficiency of repentance) is inadequate because of his deep sense of human bon-

dage. Man's natural condition is a state of captivity to powers variously described as sin, the flesh, death and astral beings. The only escape from this condition is through union with Christ. Thus in his theology the main thing that Paul wants to say about Christ is *not* that Christ is God but that Christ is the perfect heavenly Man, utterly pleasing to God and united with God, who has limitless power to co-opt believers into sharing his own heavenly blessedness.

Conservatives who claim that Paul teaches the divinity of Christ are embarrassed by the way he subordinates Christ to God. For example, in I Corinthians 15. 27-8 Paul directly contradicts the Nicene Creed. The Creed says that Christ's kingdom 'shall have no end', but Paul says that the Son will ultimately yield up the Kingdom to God. The conservatives admit that there are subordinationist elements in Paul's thought, but say they are out of keeping with the main thrust of his teaching and are perhaps a hangover from a more primitive and merely messianic view of Jesus. But really the subordination is essential, because Christ's saving power depends upon his being a perfect archetype of surrender to God. He would not be the perfect agent of God's will and the sole channel of communication between God and the world unless he were completely self-effacing

However the imagery has concealed pitfalls. Imagine that the head of some great organization, to whom his employees are very devoted, remains unseen in his sanctum, to which only his hyper-efficient secretary has access. Into the sanctum she carries reports, memos and requests for decisions, and out of the sanctum she brings a stream of directives. It all runs like clockwork. The secretary is greatly admired as being closest to the Boss, enjoying his complete confidence and being his model employee. Her influence is so great that her favour is the Boss's favour. She is his *alter ego*, people say, effectively his equal, at least so far as the day-to-day running of the business is concerned. 'That's right,' someone says, 'So far as we are concerned she *is* the Boss.' After a pause someone says, 'How do we know there is a Boss at all? Only the secretary ever sees him. He could have died years ago. It could be like those stories in which the death of a king is kept secret, and his ministers go on running the country in his name because they are afraid there will be unrest if they let it out.'

Along these lines we can imagine a series of stages in the development of Christianity. At stage one, Christ is God's perfect servant, as in Peter's Jerusalem church. At stage two, Christ is sole universal mediator, as in Paul and most vividly in the imagery of the epistle to the Hebrews, which follows my parable closely. The jargon word for this outlook is 'christocentrism'. Stage three is the affirmation of Christ's coequal divinity at Nicea. Stage four is the claim that so far as we are concerned Christ *is* God, for there is no knowledge of God or way to God apart from him. He isn't the only God there is, but our situation is such that it is as if he were the only God there is. Some forms of Protestantism say this, and the jargon name for it is 'christomonism'. Finally at stage five there is a rapid slide from various forms of 'Christian Atheism', 'Jesuolatry' and so on to outright atheism.

Some of those who question the coequal divinity of Christ do so because we believe that modern Christianity is slipping rapidly through the later stages of this sequence. So we want to return to Jesus' own message about God which started the whole thing off.

To return to St Paul, he is only at stage two, but he has already moved a very long way from Jesus and the question arises of how he has done it. Two steps between Jesus and Paul raise particular difficulties for us. The first is the post-Easter acclamation of Jesus as exalted Messiah. Here we are involved in the world of eschatological belief, a very difficult world for moderns to enter. Enthroned as Lord and Christ, Jesus had already come into his messianic kingdom in a hidden and heavenly way and it would be only a little while before it irrupted on to earth.

The second step is the identification of this exalted Jesus

with a pre-existent intermediary being, whether called the Wisdom of God, the Word of God, the Son or whatever. The point is that to speak of Christ as active in the Old Testament period (I Corinthians 10.1-13), and even as the one through whom God made the world (I Corinthians 8.6), requires a *prior* belief in an intermediary for Christ to be identified with. We do not have that prior belief.

There is a series of steps in the argument:

(*i*) Wisdom is God's heavenly companion.

(*ii*) Through Wisdom God made the world.

(*iii*) Jesus is exalted as Christ.

(*iv*) Jesus as Christ is now God's companion.

(*v*) Jesus is now to God as Wisdom is to God.

(*vi*) Jesus Christ *is* the Wisdom of God.

(*vii*) Through Christ God made the world.

In this way we may try to reconstruct the train of thought by which Paul reached his ideas, but how can we possibly share them?

Finally, conservatives who argue that Paul, at least by implication, believes in the divinity of Christ point to the doxological formulae that he uses so often, especially in beginning and ending his letters. They are forms of words that have the flavour of liturgy. The letter to the Galatians begins with a typical one:

Grace to you and peace from God the Father and our Lord Jesus Christ, who gave himself for our sins to deliver us from the present evil age, according to the will of our God and Father, to whom be the glory for ever and ever. Amen.

And it ends:

The grace of our Lord Jesus Christ be with your spirit, brethren. Amen.

The words certainly do not imply the divinity of Christ, but equally certainly they set the invocation of his name in the context of worship. They may express an embryonic belief in Christ's divinity. *God the Father* and *our Lord Jesus Christ* are certainly not yet spoken of as *God the Father* and *God the Son*, but we can see how they one day may be.

## 5.8 *John*

Of all the books in the New Testament the only one that can confidently be called incarnational in outlook is St John's gospel. Here alone Jesus is presented not just as being, but as knowing himself to be personally identical with a pre-existent heavenly being. Jesus is the incarnation of the Word or Son of God.

Dr Frances Young in a recent essay points out that in the prologue (1.1-18) it is not clear how far the Word of God is thought of as a distinct personal being. We might say that the Lord Chief Justice 'incarnates' the majesty of the Law, but the majesty of the Law is not a distinct personal being. Jesus might be revelation incarnate, or God's will and purpose embodied, in some such metaphorical sense. That is true, but in the body of the gospel God's Son is undoubtedly a pre-existent personal being and Jesus knows himself to be that being.

But is God's Son himself God? The old King-ambassador pattern of thinking is still influential, and the Son's dependence upon the Father and obedience to the Father are still very strongly stressed. In that sense there is still subordination. The Son says that 'the Father is greater than I' (14.28), a line which greatly impressed the third-century theologian Origen; and Jesus more than once goes so far as to say that God the Father is the only God, as in 17.3.

Yet the Christ of the Fourth Gospel is surely more than a created heavenly companion of God. He is divine. So I believe the fairest conclusion is that he is a subordinate divine being, God of Very God, the eternal Father's image and offspring. Elements of more primitive theology abound in the gospel, but the main tendency of its teaching is close to what was believed in Eastern Christianity just before the Council of Nicea.

This doctrine of Christ is purchased at a heavy price. It is broadly docetic, especially in the discourses of Jesus, which resemble the oracles of a gnostic redeemer. The historical Jesus has vanished almost without trace, and the echoes of his characteristic ways of speaking are faint and few. The tone of the book is anti-Jewish.

Yet historical Christianity has relied very heavily on St John's gospel for its picture of Jesus. Many Christians have claimed that St John's gospel is full of spiritual wisdom and reveals Christianity's inner meaning more profoundly than any other book. By contrast, the book seems to many Jews to show the route by which Christianity increasingly escaped into fantasy.

## 5.9 *Conclusions*

Twenty years ago Professor Oscar Cullmann, in *The Christology of the New Testament*[15], said that the New Testament writers are interested not so much in Christ's 'nature' or 'person' as in his work. What concerns them is the part he plays in the drama of salvation, the task he performs. Their language is religious and practical rather than speculative or metaphysical.

That is one way of putting the conclusion to which we are led. There are many other ways of putting it. We could say, for example, that the New Testament always speaks of 'the Son of God' (task) and never of 'God the Son' (status). The very few texts in which Jesus seems to be designated 'God' are almost all of them disputable. Professor Wiles says with characteristic mildness and accuracy that 'the text of the New Testament points in a much less direct way to the idea of incarnation than it has been thought to do during most of Christian history'.

The full coequal deity of Jesus is nowhere taught in the

New Testament. In a less strict sense, divinity *may* be predicted of Jesus in a number of texts, such as John 1.1; 1.18 (disputed: see RSV), 20.28; Hebrews 1.8f. (which hinges on a loose Old Testament ascription of divinity to the King of Israel); Romans 9.5 (disputed: see RSV); Titus 2.13 (disputed: see RSV); and II Peter 1.1 (uncertain: see RSV).

Three things can be said about the tendency towards teaching Jesus' divinity. First, when exalted to Lordship Jesus becomes irradiated with God's glory and so is seen as having a participated or communicated divinity, which leads us back again to the sense in which an ambassador is royal. Because of the greatness of his commission and his representative function he may, in his performance of that function, be accorded royal honours.

Does the New Testament go further than that? It is doubtful, but in any case the second observation is that the closer people came to affirming Jesus' full deity the further away they moved from the historical reality of Jesus himself. Jesus himself obstinately remains a devout Jew who spoke not of himself but of God, and was wholly committed to a faith, a message and an outlook which excludes incarnational doctrine. The idea of his divinity could only be reached through a considerable evolution away from his own message and outlook.

Thirdly, and most significantly of all, the incarnation is not a clear, indisputable primary datum of Christianity but a 'theory' or 'model' devised by men to account for the primary data. Being thus man-made it is in principle disputable, like all theories.

Sophisticated conservatives who are aware of the evidence and the problems concede this point, but go on to argue that the doctrine of the incarnation is still the best theory. It is impossible to do justice to the greatness of what has happened in Christ except by using incarnational language.

These conservatives acknowledge that the early church's definitions in the age after Nicea are in some ways unsatisfactory and need revision. They also acknowledge that Christianity is an offshoot of Judaism and has a deep historical obligation to try to express itself in a way that is compatible with Jewish faith and religious values. But they still say that we must end up with some form of incarnational doctrine.

If someone like me objects that incarnational doctrine is obviously a secondary mythological overlay which conceals a loss of contact with the real Jesus, they retort that the greatness of what happened in Christ took a long time to sink in. It took many decades for people to realize that Jesus had been nothing less than God incarnate.

I answer that in that case it is very odd that the truth about Jesus should be something that he himself would have found bizarre and incomprehensible, a doctrine first reached by people who had largely lost touch with his message and outlook because they had become completely cut off from the Jews.

It is replied that the church has settled these questions and that my opinion is so eccentric and so great a departure from the historic faith that it need not be considered seriously.

I reply that modern historical-critical study of Christian origins has created a new situation. Theology written before 1800 is now of only limited relevance. There has been a Reformation before, and we cannot rule out in advance the possibility that a new one is needed.

And so the argument goes back and forth. It is clear that there is a very complex cumulative case on both sides.

# 6

# Weighing the Traditional Arguments

Preachers still use a wide range of traditional arguments in support of Jesus' divinity. Some of them are obviously invalid, like the old argument from Jesus' fulfilment of prophecy. Since the Old Testament nowhere expects an incarnation of God, the fact (if it be a fact) that Jesus comprehensively fulfils Old Testament expectations cannot be sufficient to prove that he is God incarnate. But some of the other arguments can be and have been updated to take account of biblical criticism, and therefore deserve a brief review.

## 6.1 *From Jesus' filial consciousness*

Christians used to think of Jesus as being consciously God incarnate. But when we understand him as a Jew in the context of his own time, it is clear that he cannot have thought himself identical with the God he believed in and prayed to. And in fact, when (as it must be) John's gospel is set aside, when we have accepted the difficulty of making *any* psychological statements about Jesus, and when we have examined the evidence, then it is clear that we have no reason to think of Jesus as considering himself to be divine. His message is not about himself, but about God.

More cautiously, though, it is still claimed by some that he shows a 'unique filial consciousness'. It is said that he spoke of God as Father with an intimacy and immediacy unprecedented in Judaism. The items of evidence that are produced include the word *Abba*, Father (indirectly attested by St Paul, as well as in the gospels), the evidence of Jesus' prayers, and perhaps the hymn in Matthew 11.25-7 (= Luke 10.21f.).

The cogency of this argument tends to melt away on closer inspection. The hymn is of questionable authenticity, and in any case does not have to be read as claiming divinity, for there is a big jump between 'unique sonship' and 'divinity'. The picture of Jesus as a man of prayer is derived largely from St Luke, and it seems clear that Luke put in his references to Jesus at prayer in order to edify his readers. As for the son-father view of man's relation to God, it is of course deeply embedded in Jewish tradition. Israel in general and the King of Israel in particular were in a unique relation of sonship to God.

But suppose it to be true that Jesus was a man of outstanding personal devotion, who did first introduce the word *Abba* for speaking to God, it cannot possibly follow that Jesus *must* be God incarnate. There have been many outstanding saints and religious innovators who were obviously just human and no more than human. So even if the claims it makes about Jesus' filial consciousness are true, this argument can scarcely be sufficient to show that Jesus must be divine.


## 6.2 *From Jesus' claims*

The picture of Socrates that Plato gives in his dialogues is sometimes very unappealing. Socrates is so overwhelmingly superior to his interlocutors, plays with them, mocks them, exposes them and torments them with such consummate ease that one begins to sympathize with his enemies. Plato is a great literary artist, but in writing his dialogues he is so keen to pay his tribute to Socrates' originality and force of mind that he makes Socrates speak in ways that it would surely be wrong to attribute to the historical Socrates.

Rather similarly, in the gospels and above all in St John's gospel Jesus is pictured as speaking in ways that are historically unimaginable. It would be impossible to film or stage the discourses and dialogues of St John's Jesus realistically, because one who speaks like that cannot be portrayed as a convincing human being. One human being cannot look another in the eye and say, 'I am the Way, the Truth and the Life.' Nor, to take a synoptic example, could he say, 'Take my yoke upon you and learn from me; for I am gentle and lowly in heart, and you will find rest for your souls.' When in the nineteenth century people acquired the historical imagination and the novel became the dominant literary form, it was clear to everybody, and even to the orthodox, that a Jesus who talks like that is imaginatively difficult.

The orthodox response was to develop and use the famous 'mad, bad or God' argument. Yes, it was said, Jesus' gran-diose language about himself does present a difficulty. One who talks like that must be either insane, or a wicked imposter, or God. But the supreme wisdom and goodness which Jesus elsewhere shows rules out the possibilities of insanity or wickedness. We are forced to accept that he is God and is right so to speak of himself.

The argument is still popular and is used by evangelical apologists, but it makes a disturbing admission. It wants to continue to take Jesus' theological teaching literally as words spoken by the historical Jesus, but it admits that it is a moral impossibility for a normally sane human being to speak like that. So Jesus is abnormal in some way: he is either insane or evil or God. The conclusion reached is that he is God, but a corollary of the whole argument is that the incarnate God does indeed speak in ways that are incompatible with normal human goodness and sanity.

So if the mad, bad or God argument is sound, then docet-ism is true. Jesus was not perfectly human.

It comes as a great relief when biblical criticism frees one from this dilemma. The theological teaching of Jesus about himself should not be understood as words of the historical Jesus, but as a literary device. It expresses beliefs about Jesus held in the communities from which the gospels come. Just as

Plato's admiration for Socrates affects the way he represents
Socrates as speaking and behaving, so the evangelists' beliefs
about Jesus affect the way they represent him as speaking
and behaving. In both cases we have to make allowances.

In view of all this, arguments based on Jesus' claims have to
be revised considerably if they are still to be put forward.
Direct exalted claims on his own behalf are not to be expected
and according to the specialists are not in fact to be found.
Nevertheless, a careful reading of the synoptic gospels does
give a strong impression of a very forceful and authoritative
character who took the very highest view of the strange task
to which he gave himself. Jesus did not just preach the Kingdom of God: as was customary with Jewish prophecy, his
language was in some way self-fulfilling. He was bringing in
the reality which he proclaimed. His hearer's response to his
message about the Kingdom of God was a decision for or
against God. Our modern nominalism, typical of a scientific
culture, leads us to separate a man, his words, and the things
he is talking about; but ancient language was often different,
and especially for the Jews. For them language was a sacred
thing, charged with divine power. If Jesus' words were bringing in the Kingdom of God you could almost say that Jesus'
words were acts of God.

Along these lines, then, the argument from Jesus' claims
might be presented in a more accurate and up-to-date form.
Jesus said that the hour of decision had come and in the
words in which he called for a decision for God, God was
calling upon Israel for a decision. So in Jesus' voice God's
voice is heard. Jesus then is God's Word or call to men incarnate.

There is a good deal of force in an argument along these
lines. But it represents Jesus as a supreme prophet of God,
rather than as God incarnate: and indeed 'Prophet' is the
oldest and best-attested title of Jesus. His utterance had the
same kind of numinous charge and God-revealing quality as
prophetic utterance, and like prophetic utterance it

demanded a practical response to the revelation of God's will and demand that it mediated.

What are the implications of this for present-day belief? If today a reader of the gospels studies Jesus' words and finds that they still have God-revealing and life-changing power, then that modern reader is entitled to say that Jesus is a prophet of God. And if there is a quality of religious ultimacy or finality in the effect of Jesus' words on his modern reader, then that reader may call Jesus the final prophet in whom God is finally revealed. This would be a modern equivalent of the primitive eschatological finality. Jesus' words are still felt to have final religious authority which cannot be surpassed. They articulate in human words, and they engineer, a religiously final encounter with God. But all this (which I happen to believe) does not actually require one to affirm that Jesus is in his own person God incarnate. Indeed, devotion to Jesus' *person* as God incarnate may have the unfortunate side-effect of distracting attention from the very thing to which he gave his whole life, namely the reality that his words show.

## 6.3 *From Jesus' deeds*

Arguments from Jesus' miracles to his divinity are of doubtful validity because the miracles ascribed to him are so closely modelled upon miracles attributed to Old Testament figures such as Elijah and Elisha. Elisha multiplies food and heals the sick, and Elijah ascends to heaven and bestows God's spirit upon his follower, but nobody thinks of arguing that these men were therefore incarnations of God.

More seriously, the miracle-stories connected with Jesus are theological creations of the early church precisely designed to express its faith. So a good interpreter will get out of them neither more nor less than what the early church put into them: Jesus is the one appointed by God to bring in the Kingdom of God, a time when the dead will be raised, the sick will be healed, and there will be universal plenty and feasting in a transformed and perfected world. The powers Jesus wields are not his own but God's, and similar powers are promised to his disciples. They too will heal the sick, cast out demons and so on. Thus even in the terms of that particular thought-world it seems a misinterpretation to regard Jesus' miracles as proofs of his divinity. As he and his followers saw it, the miracles were really proofs that the Kingdom of God was indeed dawning.

In any case a modern must be sceptical or at the very least agnostic about miracles, because history does not admit miracles. A historian weighing the evidence must presuppose some general picture of how the world works, how human nature works, what is likely to happen and what is not likely to happen and so on. He must assume that people need food each day, that it takes a certain time to walk a certain distance, that people generally act 'in character', that rulers and military commanders make decisions that they believe will strengthen the state and win battles, and so forth. Miracles break the ordinary rules of evidence. If *anything* can happen, one cannot make a rational judgment about what is *likely* to have happened. So historical method is simply unable to handle miracles.

Fortunately, in the case of the New Testament miracles it is to a considerable extent possible to explain the nature and function of the miracle-story in theological and literary terms. If we take the stories one by one and show in each case why the writer told it, what convictions it expresses and why he chose this particular way of expressing them, then the question of historicity largely evaporates.

What of the case of the resurrection of Jesus? It is sometimes argued that this is a unique occurrence, unparalleled in history, that reveals Jesus' divinity. But that is not what it meant to the New Testament writers. In the biblical world of ideas many resurrections either occur or are hoped for, and the one who rises does not prove his own divinity by raising himself: he is raised by God. The New Testament does not teach that Jesus raised himself, but that God raised him, and it does not regard his resurrection as a unique event proving Jesus' divinity but rather as the beginning and the promise of a general resurrection. Matthew even says that many Jewish saints were raised from the dead at the time of Jesus' death (27.51-4). Whatever the resurrection was, it was not seen as certifying the incarnation but as promising that Jesus was Lord in the new age.

A number of other arguments are based on particular graces, virtues or powers ascribed to Jesus. His sinlessness or moral perfection is one such quality. It is claimed that Jesus' moral perfection is unique in history. There is some reliance here on the doctrine of original sin, for Jesus' sinlessness can only be called supernatural against the background of a general belief that all other human beings are naturally sinful: but in any case how could we ever have sufficient evidence? It may be that as a man of God, a moral teacher of great original-ity and force, and a saint and martyr, Jesus has no equal. Maybe Jesus is the greatest of all men, but how do you move from 'Jesus is the greatest of men' to 'Jesus is God incarnate'?

Recognizing these difficulties, many writers put the claim in much more general terms, saying only that God was uni-quely at work in the whole Christ-event, from the Baptism of John to the birth of the church. But this is rather like saying that God was at work in the whole Exodus-event from the birth of Moses to the giving of the Law on Mount Sinai, or that God was at work in the birth of Islam. It falls well short of affirming the incarnation.

## 6.4 *From Christian tradition and experience*

St Vincent, a monk who lived on the island of Lérins in the early fifth century, laid down a threefold test of truth for Christian doctrine. You should accept, he said, what has been believed 'everywhere, always and by all'. The true faith is oecumenical or universal, it is traditional in that it is what has been handed down from the apostles, and it is agreed by the common consent of the faithful. By these tests, many feel, it is obvious that the incarnation is a constitutive element of Christian faith. So much devotion has gathered round it, so many people have believed it for so long and the values associated with it have become so precious that it has become a massive fact that cannot be shaken by the niggling historical analysis of a few theologians. The divinity of Christ is a subject on which the church has made up its mind and cannot change its mind.

The incarnation doctrine certainly does meet *two* of St Vincent's three conditions. With a few exceptions it is, or at any rate has been, believed oecumenically by common consent. By and large it has been believed – since the fourth century at least – everywhere and by all. But as we have seen there is considerable doubt about whether it meets the third condition, of having *always* been believed ever since the apostles. It now seems that the original Jewish church saw Jesus as the exalted Messiah, and that the belief in his divinity developed slowly in the Gentile church.

The development of belief in Jesus' divinity was gradual. The first step was to identify him with a pre-existent heavenly being, and so far as we can tell it was taken by St Paul in the mid-fifties. The last step was officially to proclaim Jesus' full coequal and coeternal deity as God the Son, of one substance with the Father, incarnate; and it was taken in 325. So the development and very slow clarification of belief in Jesus' divinity lasted from 55 to 325, and then continued through the great Councils that followed. In the early stages, while Jewish ways of thinking still prevailed, Jesus' divinity was something communicated to him by the greatness of his appointment, and was rather like the sense in which an ambassador is royal. Next, he came to be seen as a subordinate divine being linking God with the world. Finally he was declared fully coequal with God the Father. But the shades of meaning and the changes of idiom are very fine and there will always be room for disagreement about just how it happened. Some key phrases, like the phrase 'Son of God', continued in use throughout while their meaning was gradually shifting, and this helped to disguise the development that was taking place. The Fathers of the fourth century believed they were merely clarifying and not departing from the original apostolic faith, and since they thought St John's gospel preserved Jesus' own words they believed that Jesus had himself taught the faith that they were defining.

Today it seems rather different, and it is hard to deny a real development of doctrine. But those who use the argument from Christian tradition and experience will still want to claim that the development was right and had to take place as it did. Maybe Jesus did not claim to be God incarnate, and maybe the first generation of Jewish Christians could not articulate the full meaning of what had happened. Certainly the intellectual task of reconciling the incarnation with monotheistic faith was daunting and had to take a very long time. But in the end the church made up its mind, and the church is right. Its faith is now verified by experience, tradition and consent and is too deep-rooted to be shifted.

This argument has some weight, but it also has some dangers. Appeals to tradition, experience and large numbers may be psychologically reassuring, but their logical force is limited. It is a well-known fact that belief shapes experience and then experience in turn seems to confirm belief. Every religious tradition produces a felt truth in that way: that is how religions keep going. But this self-confirming character of faith is a poor guide to truth. Would we be willing to say that the more exotic excesses of the cult of Mary have also verified themselves in this way?

There used to be an argument from tradition and consent for the existence of God. It was said that belief in God must be true because it has been so widely accepted for so long, and those who so argued could at least point to the fact that belief in God figures in a great many religions and philosophies.

But nobody today would dare to claim that this is a strong argument for the existence of God. The corresponding argument for the divinity of Jesus, which is believed in only one religion, must surely be even weaker. There are other religions, such as Islam and Judaism, which notice Jesus but deny his divinity. What about *their* tradition and consent?

Furthermore, those who claim that the incarnation is so strongly verified by Christian experience and consent that historical criticism of Christian origins cannot shake it run into trouble. For they are saying that Christian doctrine is now logically independent of its original historical moorings and has floated free. But if the doctrine of the incarnation can be validated without appeal to the historical Jesus, then Christianity ceases to be about *him* and becomes an autonomous myth of salvation. Then what happens to the incarnation? If you are to believe the incarnation at all, it must be anchored historically. And you cannot eat your cake and have it. The incarnation cannot be both anchored in history and logically independent of history. Many of the leading theologians of the twentieth century tried to have it both ways. But they cannot.

On the other hand suppose we ask, 'What facts about Jesus could possibly force us to believe that he is God incarnate?' The various supernatural qualities that he has in the gospels are closely modelled on Old Testament precedents, so they are not sufficient. The most they can show, even if they are historical, is that he is a supremely charismatic man of God, wielding powers and possessing graces given him by God. What additional facts could possibly force us to cross the gulf between 'Jesus is a supremely charismatic man of God' and 'Jesus is God incarnate'?

Sören Kierkegaard (1813-1855) saw the correct answer: None! He was the first to see that there is an unbridgeable gulf between *any* producible facts and arguments and the stupendous paradox of the incarnation. Yet he still believed it, even though he saw clearly that there could be no evidence or arguments for it.

Shall we join him in saying that the incarnation is a revealed truth before which our presumptuous intellects must bow? We cannot even say that, for where is it revealed? What is the evidence that it has been revealed?

# 7

# Analogies in Other Religions

## 7.1 *The problem*

That there are some notable analogies between Christian
ideas about Christ and things to be found in other religions is
obvious enough. The question is: What conclusions do we
draw from them? Sceptics sometimes talk as if the mere existence of a parallel is highly significant and shows Christian
doctrines to be untrue without further argument. Believers
are equally illogical, sometimes denying the parallels, and
then flying to the opposite extreme and arguing that of course
innumerable parallels are only to be expected because Christianity sums up and fulfils all other religions.

These inconsistencies seem to arise from the tension between two different themes in Christianity, one exclusive and
revelationist, the other universal and all-fulfilling.

In its revelationist mood, Christianity claims to possess the
only true and final revelation from God. Revelation surely
implies the disclosure by God of things that people could not
otherwise have found out. So when the idea of revelation is
being stressed all the emphasis is on the uniqueness of biblical and Christian ideas. No other religion is quite like the
Jewish religion and no other God like the God of Israel. The
covenant between Israel and God, the voice of the prophets,
Jesus' communion with God as Father and his moral teaching, and the typically Christian doctrines of the Trinity, the
incarnation, the atonement and the resurrection – all these
are claimed to be unprecedented. The novelty and uniqueness are taken as indicating that here a special revelation from
God is being given.

But then more research is done, and the supposed uniqueness seems to melt away. The Moabite Stone in the Louvre
seems to show that Moabite religion was virtually identical
with Israelite religion; prophecy and all other Israelite religious institutions are paralleled elsewhere; it becomes hard to
specify what is unique in Jesus and his message; other triads
and trinities and other incarnations are quoted; and people
point out other instances of dying and rising gods, and of
belief in redemptive suffering and divine self-sacrifice.

Now it begins to look as if the biblical and Christian tradi-
ton, far from being unique and autonomous, is in fact very
eclectic. All through its 3000-year history it has been borrow-
ing and assimilating. So the apologist hastily changes his
tack, and says that Christ is 'the desire of the nations', in
whom are realized the hopes and yearnings of all cultures.
Parallels are only to be expected.

The sceptics then retort that history shows that modern
Christianity is a kind of museum of religious history and
human religious psychology. Everything which is to be found
there can be explained by the historian. It did not drop out of
the sky; it is all man-made. There is nothing supernatural
about it.

These cross-currents of argument affect the question of the
incarnation in Christianity. For it is beyond doubt that the
incarnation doctrine did develop historically, and developed
in a culture where apparent parallels to Christian ideas
abounded on every side. Suppose we make use of these
parallels in constructing a historical explanation of the rise of
belief in the incarnation: what bearing, if any, does all this
have on the question of truth?

The search for an answer to this question will be made a
little easier if we distinguish two kinds of parallel.

## 7.2 *Dying and rising gods*

According to the old North European mythology there is a

great ash tree, Yggdrasil, at the centre of the world. It is a tree of life and of knowledge, and also a gallows, for here Odin, Father of gods and men, once voluntarily sacrificed himself. 'For nine nights, wounded by my own spear, consecrated to Odin, myself sacrificed to myself, I remained hanging from the tree.' By this act Odin gained wisdom and power to overcome evil forces, and also his own rejuvenation.

The theme of the dying and rising god is found all around the Near East in antiquity. He is often a vegetation-god, whose festival is held in the springtime. He is associated with a powerful woman-figure, his consort, who may search out his corpse and restore it to life, and his myth may include a descent into Hades. Such figures include Osiris in Egypt, Tammuz in Mesopotamia, Attis in Phrygia and Adonis in Phoenicia.

Ideas of divine incarnation are particularly common in India, the best known being the nine *avatars* of Vishnu. When the balance of good and evil is disturbed and the evil grows too great, Vishnu becomes incarnate to restore the proper order. The eighth *avatar*, Krishna, is the most popular. Folk-tale themes reminiscent of the gospels crop up in his myth, as when he is delivered from violent death in infancy and a Massacre of the Innocents takes place.

Finally, at the beginnings of civilization all over the world we find the institution of divine kingship. The King is believed to be a god, or descended from the gods.

What do parallels such as these amount to? Few people would claim much in the way of direct historical influence. The most that can be said is that there is perhaps a universal human religious psychology that across the world throws up similar patterns – appearances of a god in human form, incarnations, marvellous births, miracles, divine kingship, the death and resurrection of a god and his ascent to heaven.

There is some force in this idea. For example, Islam is in principle highly resistant to ideas of incarnation. Yet the pre-existence of Mohammed has been taught in Islam, and he has been regarded as the Logos. 'I need hardly add', comments R. A. Nicholson, 'that Mohammed gave the lie direct to those who would have thrust this sort of greatness upon him: his apotheosis is the triumph of religious feeling over historical fact'.[16] If it happened in the case of Mohammed, then it would seem possible to argue that it also occurred in the case of Jesus. There are many examples of something of great religious importance being declared to be pre-existent in Heaven. It happened not only with Mohammed but also with the Qu'ran; and it happened not only with Jesus, but also with the Torah. It may be that the rise of belief in Jesus' pre-existence can be partly explained along these lines.

Thus the first class of parallels are ones which perhaps indicate the workings of human religious psychology projecting similar ideas at different times and places.

## 7.3 *Divine men*

The second class of parallels are those where some direct historical influence upon incarnational belief may be claimed. In the fifth essay in *The Myth of God Incarnate* Dr Frances Young reviewed some of the evidence from classical antiquity. It was common for rulers to be given the same titles as were later given to Jesus – God, Son of God, Saviour – and the political ideology of kingship was close to developed Christian belief about the status of Jesus. Legend told of many outstanding men that they had been fathered by gods upon human mothers: Plato and Alexander were two such. Many wandering religious teachers claimed and were believed by their followers to be gods, and the idea that gods might appear on earth in human form was commonplace. Dr Young concludes that the indications are that the developed Christian beliefs about Jesus 'evolved from a vast range of expectations and concepts, images and speculations that were present in the culture'.[17]

The obvious objection so far is that though there was

indeed a popular tendency to pay divine honours to almost any outstanding individual, it was also the subject of ridicule. It was not a serious religious phenomenon.

But many other things can be pointed to as well. In the mystery religions people sought salvation by union with dying-and-rising gods, and Gnostic teachers told stories of heavenly figures who had descended to earth to impart secret knowledge; and these certainly were serious religious movements which could and did interact with Christianity.

In reply it is said that the first steps towards the doctrine of the incarnation were taken while Christianity was still overwhelmingly Jewish in outlook, and Jews would not have had anything to do with Gnosticism, mystery-religions or wandering pagan 'divine men'. However, Judaism at the time of the rise of Christianity was not only a pure and rational prophetic monotheism. It managed to tolerate a positively Californian variety of fanciful and eccentric speculations. In the Old Testament itself God and angels appear on earth in human form, and outstanding men are exalted to heaven. Speculative developments of these ideas could become very luxuriant. Philo's Logos was a heavenly Man and Son of God, and there is a quasi-incarnation of the Logos in Moses. Enoch is raised to heaven and transformed into the great angel Metatron, who sits by God. Jacob could be seen as a super-angelic firstborn of God.

Such ideas seem certainly to have influenced Christianity, for they repeatedly crop up in pre-Nicene thought about Christ.[18]

Finally, a point so obvious that it is easy to miss is that the gospels are packed with Old Testament allusions and quotations which model the story of Jesus on Old Testament prototypes. So the impulse to mythicize and elaborate the figure of Jesus by drawing on available religious ideas and symbols was very strong from the outset. If it was present in the first two generations – as it demonstrably was – then presumably it continued to be present.

## 7.4 *Conclusions*

But now, what does all this amount to? Everyone admits that a number of old theories of the rise of incarnational belief have been given up, and everyone admits that our knowledge of the first two centuries of Christianity is very incomplete. But at the same time it seems in principle possible (even if nobody can yet actually do it) that someone might produce a fairly full historical explanation of the rise of belief in the divinity of Christ. It was a historical process, we have some evidence and a little more may turn up, and historical processes can – to some extent – be explained by historians. Suppose it were done: what bearing would that have on the *truth* of belief in the incarnation?

Conservative believers could still say that the doctrine is true. They could make two points: they could say that it was by an inner necessity within the faith that its development drove in this direction, and they could say that it was by divine providence that all the ideas needed were lying about in the Jewish and Graeco-Roman cultural environment.

I think these replies are perfectly fair. For suppose that orthodox Christian doctrine is actually true. There is but one God in three persons, and this God wishes to reveal himself to men. How is he to do it? He does it in two stages. First he drills monotheism into their heads and then he gives a veiled revelation of his tripersonal nature, arranging to do so in a cultural setting which has the advantage of being highly pluralistic in religion and speculative in philosophy. In a dim way the revelation is understood from the outset, but it takes over 300 years to articulate it fully.

This theory uses the old idea of the 'Preparation for the Gospel', and is not negligible. Its main weakness is that it postulates a kind of divine continuity, coherence and necessity in the process of development – the kind of claim that is often made by Roman Catholics on behalf of the history of their own church. We might well argue that it is incompatible with the modern understanding of history to suppose that a hidden hand guides its course in this way.

But the conservative will say, 'In that case so much the worse for your "modern understanding of history"! If we believe in God at all, we must suppose that he guides events.'

So the conservative is not defeated yet. He will only be really badly shaken if it can be demonstrated that the development went badly wrong, and issued in a doctrine incompatible with both the Jesus who started it all off and the God he believed in. I think such a distortion *did* occur, because the world-view and values built into the developed theology of Christendom are so very different from those of Jesus and the first generation. By the time of the Council of Chalcedon the divine Christ had largely buried the historical Jesus, and it is hard to see why God should have arranged for *that* to happen!

# 8

## Problems of Reconstruction

### 8.1 *Neo-orthodoxy*

The problems, arguments and counter-arguments that we have surveyed in this book were almost all on the table for discussion during the first decade of this century. As usual, most of the leading thinkers who defined the issues were German-speaking academics. They used the critical historical method and their general outlook was Liberal. They were part of an immensely talented, industrious and self-assured class which truly believed itself to be in the vanguard of humanity's advance.

This German renaissance had lasted for more than a century and there were already signs that it had gone past its peak: the madness of Nietzsche, the emergence of an apocalyptic Jesus whom the liberal theologians could not handle, Romanticism becoming decadent and nationalism stupid and arrogant. The First World War finally precipitated a sharp reaction against the entire world-view of the older liberals, and a consequent refusal to accept their definitions of issues.

In theology the resulting movement was called Biblical Theology or Dialectical Theology. It reversed all the sign-posts, and rejected all the assumptions of liberalism. There is no way from men to God: the road runs only in the opposite direction, from God to man. Human reason and historical research cannot attain to religious truth: the only way to religious truth is to listen in faith and obedience to God's revelation. Theology presupposes faith: it is dogmatic proclamation and not critical guesswork. It does not start from the historical Jesus who is constructed by human judgment in the study, but from the Christ who is authoritatively preached in the pulpit.

The leading figure in this revolution was Karl Barth (1886-1968). A Calvinist in background, he reaffirmed the traditional Reformed belief that the canon of scripture is a rounded and unified dogmatic whole, the Word of God. Read in the right spirit of faith and obedience, it is found to communicate a single coherent dogmatic faith which the theologian simply spells out without adulterating it with human criticism or philosophy. The theologian is basically a preacher of biblical theology, and Barth held that scripture clearly teaches the full traditional faith of the church, including the doctrines of the Trinity and the incarnation.

We saw earlier (4.2, above) that Spinoza had already moved over from the dogmatic to the critical way of looking at the text of the Bible over 300 years ago, so Barth was rebelling against more than just nineteenth-century liberalism. He was trying to put the clock back several centuries. He could hardly deny the existence of modern history, science and philosophy, but in the field of theology and religion he demanded a reversion to precritical ways of thinking.

How could he attempt such an impossible *tour de force?* He had learnt from Kierkegaard that there is no way to knowledge of the incarnation by historical criticism and rational argument. Yet Christian faith is itself a massive fact. It cannot be man-made: it must be God-given. The Bible – and with it presumably the thousand-year stretch of history that it reflects, though Barth is unclear on this point – must be given a special privileged status as God's Word to man. Read the Bible in the right spirit and receive the truth; and if Barth has copied down what he had heard faithfully, then there is little to add.

Barth disdained the historical Jesus as a figure of little interest. For him the incarnation was revealed ideology rather than historical occurrence in any normal sense of 'historical', so that one is left wondering in what sense he believes in the incarnation at all.

The neo-orthodox theology of which Barth was the most distinguished representative has now collapsed and survives chiefly, perhaps, in Scotland. Apart from its authoritarianism, the main reason why it failed was that it tried to seal Christian thought up in a closed circle of dogmatic ideas. Barth could not take faiths other than Christianity seriously, could not do justice to the internal diversity and historically-conditioned character of the biblical books, could not deal with the cross-connections between biblical and extra-biblical ideas and events, and could not intelligibly connect theological with non-theological uses of language and ways of thinking.

So neo-orthodoxy turned out to be a blind alley. When it passed away all the old questions that it had rejected came back again, tougher than ever after decades of neglect.

## 8.2 *Evolving beyond Jesus*

The pre-1914 liberal theologians received a very bad press from the next generation. They were accused of 'historicism', belief in inevitable historical progress in accordance with laws of historical development, and charged with a facile and man-centred optimism which allowed them to think of themselves as the leading edge of history's forward movement.

If indeed they were guilty of these sins, then no doubt Barth and others were right to rebel against them. But beneath that unattractive surface was a permanent achievement which could not be rejected, the critical method and the historical imagination. During the present century, even while Barth was creating his own extraordinary system, the techniques of biblical criticism and historical research were being still further refined and the social sciences were developing rapidly. Barth's attempt to insulate theology from the problems of history and cultural change ends by making

us see them looming larger than ever. What has Barth's
Christ got to do with Jesus? Very little. What has Barth's
theology got to do with what the various biblical writers
thought they were doing when they wrote? Very little.
Barth's theology cannot do justice to the deep embeddedness
of religion in history.

One might compare modern Christianity with a city like
Paris or London which is of about the same age and has
grown over the centuries in an analogous way. What we see
today is something very different from the original tiny set-
tlement of tribesmen. Many elements in the city – buildings,
the oldest parts of the street-plan, language, institutions, customs – have roots going back into the remote past, but they
survive now as components in a way of life which belongs
wholly to the twentieth century. There is continuity, but the
things that continue do not continue quite unchanged. They
are taken up into a new and different whole in each period,
just as the same language is used in different ways in each
century.

The analogy between the church and a city is biblical and
has an attraction for Catholics. Protestantism is like a city-
state with a detailed written Constitution that cannot be
amended, but Catholicism has both the written Constitution
and a 'living voice' of authority which continually reinterprets
the Constitution in the light of new circumstances. Catholicism would therefore seem to be in a better position to admit
the reality of historical change and adjust to it. During the
nineteenth century theories of the church's development
began to appear, issuing in the end in the Modernist crisis of
the years 1900-1910.

The Catholic Modernists accepted biblical criticism even
when its conclusions were sceptical, because they believed
that human religious life must inevitably take different forms
in different ages. There are no history-transcending absolutes
because the church's dogmatic teaching is itself a product of
history, and is understood differently in different periods. So

the Modernists regarded dogmas as symbolic and culturally conditioned expressions of the religious life and aspirations of a particular time. The church's task is not to guard unchanged a body of timeless truths committed to her by Jesus Christ, but to *be* the church in its own time, relating men to God today in a way appropriate to today's conditions. If the city lives and functions today as an organic whole then the question of who first founded it and what laws he laid down is of secondary importance. Wholly unfettered biblical criticism and historical study of the church's doctrinal development will help the church to be the church today by showing the profoundly historical character of Christianity. In every age the church must be the church in a new and different way, and in an important sense the church *must* evolve beyond Jesus and leave him behind.

It has often been pointed out that the views put forward today by Dr Dennis Nineham of Keble College, Oxford somewhat resemble the ideas of the old Catholic Modernists. He strongly emphasizes the reality of cultural change, and – following Bultmann (4.8, above) – the gulf between the New Testament's world-view and ours. He does not regard the past as incomprehensible: on the contrary, he insists on the value of taking an imaginative leap into the quite different world of the New Testament writers. But we will not find anything there that we can pick up, bring back, and transplant unchanged into our own time. The most we can expect is that the adventure will, after our return, be found to have affected our imaginative and practical response to our own world.

Dr Nineham makes a telling point about the treatment of Christ in modern theology. Most preachers talk as if the Christ they preach is identical with the Jesus of history. Theologians know that this is not so, but the theories devised in the attempt to connect the modern Christ with the original Jesus have become so far-fetched and obscure as to carry no conviction outside a very small circle.

Nineham asks:

... is it any longer worthwhile to attempt to trace the Christian's everchanging understanding of his relationship with God directly back to some identifiable element in the life, character and activity of Jesus of Nazareth?

And he adds:

If ... such an attempt is made will it lead inevitably to a degree of sophistication which is unintelligible to the majority of Christians and brings the so-called christological thinking involved into disrepute? [19]

Dr Nineham's views and questions have been assailed with swear-words like 'relativism' and 'scepticism', but have not been satisfactorily answered. He is surely right to say that the Christ of present-day faith is very different from Jesus, and that the attempts of theologians to connect the two are often remarkably obscure and unconvincing.

The problem here goes back to Plato (4.9, above) who first saddled us with a sense of the disparity between eternal truth and transient fact, a tension that runs right through European culture. Committed artists make their principles clear, but are charged with not doing justice to the flux of life. Uncommitted pure artists may do justice to the flux, but are then accused of being unprincipled and nihilistic. Those who are aware of both worlds but keep them distinct are accused of 'bourgeois idealism'. How can one synthesize the temporal and the eternal, the essentially changing and the essentially unchanging? Karl Barth's theology is strong on eternal revealed truth, but does not do justice to the flux of actual historical existence. Dr Nineham certainly does justice to history, but is charged with admitting no absolutes.

## 8.3 *An inspired man*

It is sometimes said that if the idea of the incarnation be given up 'nothing is left of Christianity', because 'Jesus was either God incarnate or he was nothing'. This is a most illogical idea. It is generally agreed that the main sources which tell us what Jesus was like are the synoptic gospels, and that those three gospel-writers do not teach the doctrine of the incarnation. If the doctrine were given up those three gospels would still remain, saying just what they say now; and clearly Matthew, Mark and Luke regard Jesus as a figure of the very highest religious significance. Where everything is pinned on the doctrine of the incarnation it is easy to lose sight of the great variety of other things the New Testament says about Jesus – especially the things that are *incompatible* with the theory of incarnation.

Professor G. W. H. Lampe, in *God as Spirit*[20] makes a broad distinction between two kinds of 'model' or theory for interpreting Jesus, incarnation and inspiration, and argues in detail for the superiority of the latter. Many important religious values are better brought out by the inspiration model – the personal character of Jesus' relation to God, the moral worth and exemplary value of his work, and so on. It may well be argued that if Christ is a being different in kind from Christians, the solidarity between Christians and Christ is weakened. So far over a century there has been a long line of theologians who have treated the difference between Christ and Christians as one of degree rather than of kind, beginning with F. D. E. Schleiermacher (*The Christian Faith*, 1821-2), who regarded Jesus as being unique in the intensity of his consciousness of God.

However, theologies of this kind run into a general difficulty. Emphasizing Jesus' human solidarity with us, they pick out one or more attributes of Jesus which they hold to be of supreme value: attributes such as Jesus' consciousness of God, his faith, his obedience, his moral perfection, his experience of God's grace, his inspiration by God's Spirit and his love for others. For the argument to work we have to be historically sure, for any given quality, that Jesus really did have it, that he had it in the very highest degree, and that he had it in a way relevant to us.

But in his essay in *The Myth of God Incarnate* and elsewhere, Dr Dennis Nineham has asked some very pertinent questions about this kind of argument. It runs into some of the same difficulties as arguments for the incarnation. Our historical knowledge of Jesus is very slight. How could we ever know enough about Jesus to be sure that he was not just a good man but a *perfectly* good man; and in view of the enormous difference between his world and ours, how do we show the continuity between his goodness in his time and whatever forms of moral goodness are possible for us? Much of the modern talk about Jesus as the supreme teacher and example of altruistic love, for example, is very insecurely based in the gospel texts. Jewish values, virtues and piety in the context of Jesus' own time have a very different flavour from modern values, virtues and piety.

The problem is one that Albert Schweitzer saw long ago. There is a strong element of fantasy in the picture of Jesus as God incarnate, but there may equally be a strong element of fantasy in humanist or liberal theologies. Can modern Christianity really be convincingly connected with Jesus, or will it always be plagued by the problem of the lack of evidence and the great difference between his world and ours?

## 8.4 *Back to the real Jesus?*

Albert Schweitzer's *Von Reimarus Zu Wrede*, titled in English *The Quest of the Historical Jesus*, first appeared in 1906.[21] Schweitzer was not quite the first to say what he said, and there have been many attempts since either to qualify or to overthrow his thesis; but in the main his argument was sound. The real Jesus was a wholly Jewish figure, an eschatological prophet who was dominated by the expectation that history as we know it would very soon come to an end and the Kingdom of God would arrive.

Twentieth-century Christianity has still not recovered from

the shock, and Schweitzer's book remains the principal single cause of its somewhat demoralized state. In its heart of hearts it fears that it has been shown to be a fantasy. The first generation of believers, who saw Jesus as exalted Messiah, held a faith still compatible with him and what he had been and still expected the End very soon. But as the hope faded the faith was transformed, and the Christ of the developed church became a very different figure from Jesus. So long as the Jewish background was little known and St John's gospel was thought historical, people remained largely unaware of the problem. But now the age of innocence is past.

It is still widely assumed that the real Jesus was too strange and remote a figure to be able to exercise a real religious influence upon the modern world. But suppose we question this assumption, and look at him afresh? Is it possible to find in him something that remains of history-transcending religious significance?

I have myself attempted an argument along these lines in *Jesus and the Gospel of God* [22] and in other places. I accept the well-established Schweitzer-and-Bultmann view of Jesus, and I accept that we do not know anything for certain about his life and teaching. But the most well-established facts about him are that he taught about the Kingdom of God, and that in his teaching he used parables and similar linguistic devices. If we reflect on the rhetorical stratagems he used we see that the language is a form of action. Jesus used language to act upon his hearer, directly to show the nearness of God and incite the hearer to decide for God. The *form* of Jesus' utterance, not the *content,* is the real clue. The medium is the message: Jesus' linguistic tools reveal what it was that he sought to do and to show.

Jesus was dualistic: he makes a sharp contrast between the present world-order, ruled by Satan and heading for destruction, and the coming new reality. To pass from the old world to the new requires a kind of death and rebirth. The two worlds are so unlike that language cannot run smoothly from the old reality to the new. There has to be paradox and imaginative shock.

And Jesus had to be an eschatological prophet. Standing spiritually at the end of time, he speaks to all times because however we have constructed ourselves and our world we still have to 'die' in order to know God. Standing where he did, Jesus shows the ultimate truth about the human situation before God, and shows it in language that can be tested because it still works. His words are his work, and in his words he still lives and still relates men to God.

The God of Jesus is radically transcendent and for that very reason not remote, as is sometimes mistakenly thought, but very close, only a moment away. God can be known only by an act of the purest freedom, by which one 'turns', repents or is converted to God. Hence the highest truth of religion is that the supreme good cannot be had by any amount of worldly effort or by religiosity, but only by 'turning' or 'dying' wholly. After Jesus himself experienced this at his baptism he believed that the Kingdom was already in a hidden way present in his own ministry. By a kind of prophetic foreshortening of the future he could not do otherwise than see its full consummation as very close. And indeed one who has experienced the reality that he proclaimed is bound to agree with him: he was right and it *is* close.

Thus in my view Christianity should be much more tightly focussed upon Jesus' words than it has usually been in the past. The picturesque mythologization of Jesus, which began so early, was always in danger of falsifying him and obscuring his real message, and is in any case now obsolete.

So I claim that the real Jesus is a much more interesting and religiously-relevant figure than the divine Christ of later faith, and he has the advantage of having actually lived. In our pluralistic and critical culture we have a deep sense of transience and a longing for the transcendent. But criticism has made us aware of the merely human character of the traditional dogmatic belief-systems through which people used to think they could find God. Christendom-Christianity does not work any more. The historical Jesus is the real Christ for today.

However, it is another question whether I can persuade anyone at all to agree with me. An extremely senior theologian (a priest, like me) recently took me aside and said with deep pastoral concern, 'You know, Don, I can't understand why you're so potty about Jesus'!

## 8.5 *Jesus and the world religions*

In traditional societies religion, culture and territory were very closely linked. God or the Gods had established a sacred domain and a people to fill it. It seemed to the people that in their own sacred land and its social and religious order was the fullness of truth and sanity, cosmos amid the surrounding chaos. When you came to the frontiers of the sacred domain you approached an area where the true God's writ did not yet run, and the world was not yet fully cosmos. It was a region of demons, monsters, heathen barbarians, and idolaters with unnatural habits. It was a place where there could be no salvation, because salvation consisted in membership of the properly-constituted divine-human order. It was a noble task to serve the God and enlarge his cosmos by evangelism and war, pushing out the frontiers and driving back the demons.

Such ideas passed from primitive tribesmen to the first city states and then to many of the great religions. China and India, Islam and Christendom were all sacred domains in that sense. It is broadly true that in the past men built their world-views and their beliefs around themselves, seeing their God as the only true God, their customs and beliefs as the only right and true ones, their sacred domain as the centre of creation, and membership in their community as being the only true path to salvation. The cluster of ideas involved here has proved extraordinarily tenacious, and has survived until modern times. Ethnocentricity was a sacred obligation, and lingers on in modern nationalism.

Yet the Copernican revolution clearly marked the beginning of a different outlook. In modern times mechanical transport, huge population movements and electronic communications are gradually mixing cultural traditions which once kept themselves firmly separate. The old ethnocentric outlook, which in some contexts is still regarded as a decent and laudable 'nationalism', in other contexts comes to be seen as objectionable racialism and sectarian bigotry. The old kind of religious belief that was once such a powerful unifying force now begins to seem divisive and irrational. Internationally-minded people look on traditional faiths as survivals, ethnic folkways which have to be handled with caution lest they cause trouble. In the new global culture religion must either become itself global or be seen merely as a political nuisance and a survival from primitive times.

Professor John Hick, in *God and the Universe of Faiths*,[23] says that religious thought must go through a Copernican revolution. Instead of seeing my faith as the centre of the universe I have to learn to see God as the centre of the universe of faiths which revolve about him as the planets circle the sun. Traditional claims to possess exclusive truth, infallible scriptures and divine incarnations in one's own tradition must be seen as mythological: that is, stories told to validate the claims of a particular community. In the future the various faiths will very properly borrow from each other and begin to converge, and theologians ought to start work on a universal theology of religions.

Hick's case is strong, though I am uncertain whether recognition of the validity of other religions strictly obliges one to give up the incarnation. If God is infinitely various, might he not reveal himself by incarnation in one tradition and in some other way in another, while yet both traditions are as true as any human expression of religious truth can be? Maybe this suggestion is too farfetched, for in practice believers in the incarnation do conclude that all other religions are relatively inferior.

Many will object to Hick that his programme has been attempted before. There was ancient syncretism, which tried to meld different cults, there was the 'natural religion' of the eighteenth century, and in modern times people have sought an inner unity of the religions at the level of mysticism. Syncretistic movements like Sikhism and the Bahai (whose views resemble Hick's own) have arisen. The Bahai faith is a universal monotheism with both liberal and messianic elements which acknowledges Moses, the Buddha, Zoroaster, Krishna, Jesus and Muhammad. But the Bahai, for all its protestations, is only another sect and the case against Hick is that projects like his will always founder on the rock of the irreducible dissimilarity of religions. People will not fight for what they have in common: they only fight for their badges of distinctiveness. In every faith the real true believers are the most fanatical, intransigent, jealous, orthodox, reactionary zealots. Liberals come and go, but the fundamentalists are the real survivors and they always win in the end.

That is true, but it is all the more reason why Professor Hick's project must be attempted. If in each faith the last survivors will be a small nucleus of ultra-conservatives, then religion will in the end disappear. It is up to the liberals to prove themselves tougher.

## 8.6 *Christian personalism*

As we have seen, the current debate about the divinity of Christ is so wideranging that there are at least six points at which one can enter it.

First, there are the long-known logical and religious difficulties of the classical doctrine, which have never been wholly solved.

Secondly, the secularization of our world-picture and the growth of our knowledge in the last few centuries has made the old Christian story of salvation seem like a fairytale. What is to be done about this? Many claim that 'Myth may be the vehicle of a profound spiritual truth', but since they are unable to spell out precisely what that truth is the problem of myth remains without an agreed solution. There are two very important points *against* myth. The first is that it represents God anthropomorphically, thinking and acting like a magnified human being who inhabits a higher world; and the second is that myth is so often ethnocentric, being concerned to place a particular society at the centre of the universe as a people with a uniquely privileged status. For both these reasons there is a strong case against trying to update Christian mythology. Attempts to do it, such as Teilhard de Chardin's, have met strong (and, it seems to me, justified) objections.

Thirdly, there is the question of biblical criticism and the re-emergence of that strange figure, the historical Jesus. Much of modern theology tried to keep the doctrine of the incarnation while effectively disregarding him, which seems very paradoxical. If the arguments linking the divine Christ to the real Jesus are seen as sophistries, what is to be done? Tie Christianity strictly to the real Jesus, or let him slide back gracefully to the place where he belongs, in the remote past?

Fourthly, there is the historical reconstruction of the development of belief in the divinity of Christ, AD 51 – 451. Conservatives claim that the belief was implicit all along and others say that it was not, but gradually developed or evolved. Either way, the arguments that the early writers used are available for criticism.[24]

Fifthly, there is the manifest weakness of the standard arguments from facts about Jesus to his divinity.

Sixthly, there is the question of the religious validity of faiths other than Christianity. Is Christianity now obliged to give up the exclusive claims implied by incarnational doctrine, in order to admit that there really is true communion with God outside the church?

Appraising all these controversies, we have to work on two levels, judging each particular point of detail accurately while at the same time having regard to the overall coherence of the whole. A theologian must seek a reasonably unified religious outlook, without cheating in the fine detail of the evidence and arguments.

Because the arguments are so complex, alliances and disagreements cut across each other; but many participants in the debate share a general outlook that may be called Christian Personalism. Both 'heretics' and 'orthodox' tend to agree in saying that (*i*) God is personal and loving; (*ii*) the eternal conservation of personality is a supremely important moral and religious value; (*iii*) Jesus has a special place in God's purposes and mankind's religious history; and (*iv*) what happened in the whole event of Jesus Christ is a pledge that God is indeed personal love and will conserve human personality.

Thus in most people's view what is distinctive in Christianity is its emphasis on love and on the value of the person. In a single sentence, the gospel is that in Jesus has occurred a revelation of God's personal love for men which frees us from the fear that the universe is ultimately dead and indifferent to personal and moral values.

A somewhat similar view of the essence of Christianity is taken by Hans Küng in Germany,[25] but if we compare the two we find that Küng's Christian humanism is oriented more towards liberation, the community and politics, whereas the British version is more private, quakerish and domestic.

I am one of the few participants in the debate who questions this widely-held outlook.

The issue between those personalists who believe in the incarnation and those who do not is neatly epitomized in a dispute between Professor Lampe and Mr Hebblethwaite. Hebblethwaite says that personality requires reciprocity. If God is eternally personal there must be eternal personal distinctions within God, and the incarnation of God the Son reveals that this is so. Hebblethwaite therefore stands in the Anglican tradition that believes in a social Trinity.

Lampe thinks this is a projection, and that it is incompatible with belief in the unity of God. God participates in all human loves and enters into fellowship with men. The religious and social experience that Jesus has introduced contains within itself the assurance and the experience of the personality of God.[26]

Hebblethwaite retorts that on Lampe's account the world is necessary to God, for God needs to create persons in order to realize his own nature as personal.[27]

But Lampe can reply that God is eternal so that, from God's end as it were, God's participation in the life of creatures is eternal. Besides, the idea that earthly personal relationships need to have heavenly archetypes to validate them is a piece of naive mythology. We do not any longer need the idea that earthly things are mere shadows of things laid up in another and higher world.

This argument raises the whole question of projection. When Hebblethwaite says that the Trinity guarantees the eternal worth of the personal is he not laying himself open to the charge that his theology – and by implication, every personalist and humanist theology – is merely a projection of humanity's need for support and reassurance?

For myself, I do feel that much of modern Christianity, and *especially* orthodoxy, has become a projection of basically secular humanist and personal values. In search of pure transcendence uncontaminated by wishful thinking I have moved to an exceedingly high-and-dry view of God, and from Jesus' flesh to his words. It is complained that my religion is dehumanized to the point of emptiness. But if an ascetical and wholly dehumanized religion is indeed empty, then surely the projection-theory of religion advanced by Feuerbach, Marx, Freud, Durkheim and others is right? Whereas if I can show that a dehumanized religion still works and is real, then I can exorcize those formidable spectres.

Another question is, can the Christian personalist outlook be traced back to Jesus himself? Some would say yes. Others would admit that it cannot but say that it does not matter, for the church is a living and growing organism continually learning new truth. In theory it does not matter if the church comes to stand for values almost the opposite of what Jesus stood for. I say that Christian personalist values cannot be traced back to Jesus himself, and it *does* matter, because I want the form of our relation to God to be what Jesus showed in his words. Paradoxically, I give the historical Jesus a higher religious value than do many of the incarnationalists.

Finally there is the great issue of the Jesus of history and the divine Christ of faith, God the Son incarnate. Can the two be identified, plausibly and without sophistry? I say no, and my prime allegiance is to the Jesus of history. But there are two ways of saying yes.

Some Modernists would say that the divine Christ of faith is a being of whom we have present religious experience in the sacraments and the life of the church. This experience is traceable back to New Testament times. But gospel criticism admittedly leaves so many uncertainties that we cannot get behind the New Testament with any confidence. We just have to believe that there was a man out of whose life, death and resurrection came this new reality we now experience. To believe the incarnation is to believe that the divine Christ we now know is anchored in history somewhere beneath the pages of the New Testament. We cannot see the point at which the anchor bites into the ground. We just have to believe that it does bite.

Mr Hebblethwaite's kenotic doctrine of Christ which we introduced in Chapter 1 is a little more confident about Jesus. We do know what he was, namely an ordinary first-century Jewish man who believed in God, prayed to God and spoke to God, but was in no way conscious of *being* God. Hebblethwaite's theory simply yokes this man to God the Son. God the eternal Son has lived this life as his own incarnate life. Hebblethwaite admits that there are no facts about Jesus from which it can be validly inferred that he is God the Son incarnate, and makes a virtue of the lack of evidence. The absence of divinity-proving characteristics in Jesus only goes to show the perfection of the divine self-emptying in Jesus.

To me it seems that it is not God who is emptied, but Hebblethwaite's own theory. What evidence could count either for or against it? Is it not the case that both these versions of incarnational theology are on the point of collapse? Both admit that we have not really got the evidence any more, and both invite us to go on believing the incarnation on the authority of the church and tradition, and because it is a good thing to believe. Is that enough, or has the time come for a change of direction?

# Notes

1. From J. Stevenson, *A New Eusebius*, SPCK 1957, p. 365.

2. Stevenson, op. cit., p. 366.

3. From T. H. Bindley, *The Oecumenical Documents of the Faith*, Methuen 1899, p. 297.

4. Bindley, op. cit., pp. 269–71.

5. See A. Koyré, *From the Closed World to the Infinite Universe*, Baltimore: John Hopkins 1957, ch. II.

6. *The Song of Roland*, trans. D. L. Sayers, from stanza 266.

7. From S. Z. Ehler and J. B. Morall, *Church and State Through the Centuries*, Burnes & Oates 1954, p. 92.

8. *On Divine Revelation*, III, 13. Full text in W. M. Abbott, *Documents of Vatican II*, Chapman 1967.

9. Quoted in Horton Harris, *David Friedrich Strauss and his Theology*, Cambridge University Press 1973, p. 262.

10. William Temple, *Readings in St John's Gospel*, one-volume edition, Macmillan 1945.

11. C. H. Dodd, *Historical Tradition in the Fourth Gospel*, Cambridge University Press 1963.

12. D. E. Nineham, 'Epilogue' in John Hick (ed.), *The Myth of God Incarnate*, SCM Press 1977, pp. 186–204.

13. John A. T. Robinson and D. L. Edwards (eds), *The Honest to God Debate*, SCM Press 1963, p. 138n.

14. See H. W. Bartsch (ed.), *Kerygma and Myth*, SPCK 1955.

15. Oscar Cullmann, *The Christology of the New Testament*, SCM Press 1959.

16. R. A. Nicholson, *Studies in Islamic Mysticism*, Cambridge University Press 1921, p. 88.

17. Frances Young, in *The Myth of God Incarnate*, p. 87.

18.  See J. Danielou, *The Theology of Jewish Christianity*, Darton, Longman & Todd 1964.

19.  Nineham in *The Myth of God Incarnate*, p. 202.

20.  G. W. H. Lampe, *God as Spirit*, Oxford University Press 1977.

21.  Third edition, A. & C. Black 1954.

22.  Don Cupitt, *Jesus and the Gospel of God*, Lutterworth 1979.

23.  John Hick, *God and the Universe of Faiths*, Macmillan 1973, Fontana edition 1977.

24.  For example, M. F. Wiles, *Working Papers in Doctrine*, SCM Press 1976; G. W. H. Lampe, *God as Spirit*, Oxford University Press 1977; G. C. Stead, *Divine Substance*, Oxford University Press 1977.

25.  Hans Küng, *On Being a Christian*, ET, Collins 1977.

26.  Lampe, *God as Spirit*, pp. 138ff.

27.  See his paper in *Incarnation and Myth*, SCM Press 1979.

# *Further Reading*

I append a very short list of books, mostly published recently, which help to fill in the background to the current debate.

H.W. Bartsch (ed.), *Kerygma and Myth*, SPCK 1955
*Christian Believing*, A Report by the Doctrine Commission of the Church of England, SPCK 1976
Don Cupitt, *Jesus and the Gospel of God*, Lutterworth 1979
Michael Green (ed.), *The Truth of God Incarnate*, Hodder & Stoughton 1977
M. D. Goulder (ed.), *Incarnation and Myth*, SCM Press 1979
John Hick, *God and the Universe of Faiths*, Macmillan 1973
John Hick, *The Centre of Christianity*, SCM Press 1977
John Hick (ed.), *The Myth of God Incarnate*, SCM Press 1977
J. L. Houlden, *Explorations in Theology 3*, SCM Press 1978
G. W. H. Lampe, *God as Spirit*, Oxford University Press 1977
C. F. D. Moule, *The Origin of Christology*, Cambridge University Press 1977
D. E. Nineham, *The Use and Abuse of the Bible*, Macmillan 1976
J. A. T. Robinson, *Honest to God*, SCM Press 1963
J. A. T. Robinson and D. L. Edwards (eds), *The Honest to God Debate*, SCM Press 1963
M. F. Wiles, *The Remaking of Christian Doctrine*, SCM Press 1974
M. F. Wiles, *Working Papers in Doctrine*, SCM Press 1976

# Index of Names